T0328851

RAFFAELE MATTIOLI LECTURES

In honour of the memory of Raffaele Mattioli, who was for many years its manager and chairman, Banca Commerciale Italiana has established the Mattioli Fund as a testimony to the continuing survival and influence of his deep interest in economics, the humanities and sciences.

As its first enterprise the Fund has established a series of annual lectures on the history of economic thought, to be called the Raffaele Mattioli Lectures.

In view of the long association between the Bocconi University and Raffaele Mattioli, who was an active scholar, adviser and member of the governing body of the University, it was decided that the lectures in honour of his memory should be delivered at the University, which together with Banca Commerciale Italiana, has undertaken the task of organising them.

Distinguished academics of all nationalities, researchers and others concerned with economic problems will be invited to take part in this enterprise, in the hope of linking pure historical research with a debate on economic theory and practical policy.

In creating a memorial to the cultural legacy left by Raffaele Mattioli, it is hoped above all that these lectures and the debates to which they give rise will prove a fruitful inspiration and starting point for the development of a tradition of research and academic studies like that already long established in other countries, and that this tradition will flourish thanks to the new partnership between the Bocconi University and Banca Commerciale Italiana.

ECONOMIC LAWS
AND ECONOMIC HISTORY

RAFFAELE MATTIOLI FOUNDATION

Economic Laws
and
Economic History

CHARLES P. KINDLEBERGER

CAMBRIDGE
UNIVERSITY PRESS

Published by the Press Syndicate of the University of Cambridge
The Pitt Building, Trumpington Street, Cambridge CB2 IRP
40 West 20th Street, New York, NY 10011-4211, USA
10 Stamford Road, Oakleigh, Melbourne 3166, Australia

Edited by Giuliano Mussati

First published 1989
First paperback edition 1997

Library of Congress Cataloguing in Publication Data
Main entry under title:
Economic Laws and Economic History
(Raffaele Mattioli Lectures)
At head of title: Raffaele Mattioli Foundation.
Bibliography.
1. Economic Laws – Addresses, essays, lectures.
2. Economic History – Addresses, essays, lectures.
I. Kindleberger, Charles P.   II. Raffaele Mattioli Foundation.   III. Series
HB 3732.D43   1984   338.9   84-21366

British Library Cataloguing in Publication Data
Kindleberger, Charles P.
Economic Laws and Economic History
(Raffaele Mattioli Lectures)
1. Economics
I. Title   II. Series
ISBN 0 521 26791 9 HB
ISBN 0 521 59975 X PB

Transferred to digital printing 2004

CONTENTS

integration and the elimination of intermediary marketing steps, pp. 79-81.   6. The role of arbitrage, pp. 82-84.
7. The problem of foreign direct investment, pp. 85-86.
8. The optimum economic area, pp. 87-91.   9. Conclusions, p. 92.

PREFACE

My topic for these lectures is Economic Laws and Economic History, somewhat removed perhaps from the emphasis on the history of economic thought these lectures are supposed to have, but not entirely orthogonal. I am an historical economist, not an economic historian, by which I mean that I am interested in using history to test the validity and generality of economic laws and models. Donald McCloskey has said in praise of economic history that it can serve to produce "more economic facts, better economic facts, better economic theory, better economic policy, and better economists".[1] As a teacher, of course I subscribe to the last. In research, my interest is in better theory in the sense of more useful, more general and more relevant theories, and the discarding of that which is merely elegant but has no bearing on how people behave in an economy.

I hope in these lectures to go beyond this interest in better theory to attempt to demonstrate, what perhaps needs no demonstration, that there is no one all-purpose economic theory or model that illuminates economic history, and that for economic historians to cling to a single or central theory is misleading, and in general wrong. You will recall that Keynes once said that economists should be like dentists, by which he meant that they should view their craft modestly, and not use it to explain all the mysteries of life, in the case of dentists, or of social inter-

1. DONALD N. MCCLOSKEY, 'Does the Past Have Useful Economics?', *Journal of Economic Literature*, vol. XIV, No. 2, June 1976, pp. 434-61.

course for economists.[1] I go further and think that Keynes believed that, like dentists, we must have more than one tool in our armoury with which to analyse economic problems and events. A dentist with only one drill, or only one pair of pliers . . . I stop because the metaphor becomes disagreeable. A year ago I happened to see a silversmith at an exhibition bench with an array of 60 hammers, each slightly different from the next. He said that a jeweller might have 500 hammers, and constantly use 100 among them for very slightly different tasks. This makes the same point. The economic historian or the economist seeking to test his analysis against historical data should be prepared to put down one economic law or model, and pick up another, when the condition to be explained calls for it, and not to insist on using always the same tool. It is all very well to ascribe importance to stages of growth, backwardness, the critical role of banking, the quantity of money, property rights, other institutions, public goods, the market . . . but one should be careful not to get so caught up in a given law affecting part of the system as to think it both necessary and sufficient to explain how the world economy has arrived in its present condition.

My title is "Economic Laws and Economic History." I chose this in preference to "Economic Models and Economic History" for two reasons, one mainly cosmetic, that I have found four models which can somewhat loosely be described with the name of "laws", rather than four models. Beyond this, it is probably correct to say that laws adhere more closely to reality than models do. Some years ago at a faculty club luncheon table, a young theorist on one side of me said to our colleague on the other side that he had developed an interesting model and hoped that the latter would help him find an application for it! Models have more mathematics, of which I have none. Laws have a solid empirical base as inductive generality. At a certain rhetorical level, however, laws and models are synonymous. Say's "law" that supply creates its own demand is in reality only a

1. JOHD MAYNARD KEYNES, 'Economic Possibilities for Our Grandchildren', *Nation and Athenaeum*, 11th and 18th October 1930; reprinted in *Essays in Persuasion*, London: Macmillan, 1931; New York: Harcourt Brace & Co., 1932; also in *The Collected Writings of John Maynard Keynes*, vol. IX, London: Macmillan, 1972, p. 321-32.

model that can be either confronted with other models, such as Keynes' model that demand creates its own supply, or refuted with historical counterexamples. The merchants of Rouen in France, for example, did not sell all the textiles they brought to the annual fairs at Caen and Guilbray, as Say's law and the Walrasian model would call for. Each year between 1705 and 1781 they regularly brought back to their workshops and warehouses an average of 25 to 30 per cent of the woollen textiles they took to market to sell, 14 per cent at the minimum, 58 per cent at the maximum.[1] The Stolper-Samuelson theorem that the scarce factor benefits from tariffs no matter in what industry it is engaged in has been tested against the view of Cairnes, based on non-competing groups, and found less able to explain the positions actually taken by capital and labour on particular tariff issues.[2]

I trust I can be forgiven if I depart from my old interests in international economics, the law of comparative advantage, price-specie-flow mechanism, factor-price equalization and the like, though these hardy perennials bloom briefly in the last lecture on the law of one price. The object of the exercise is to discuss a few laws deeply rooted in observed reality that have powerful explanatory power for some, but not for all economic history, to show that eclecticism rather than an all-encompassing system of interpretation is the wiser attitude to bring to the study of the economic past.

1. PIERRE DARDEL, *Commerce, industrie et navigation à Rouen et au Havre au XVIIIe siècle. Rivalité croissante entre ces deux ports*, Rouen: Société libre d'Émulation de la Seine-Maritime, 1966, pp. 54-5.

2. STEPHEN P. MAGEE, 'Three Simple Tests of the Stolper-Samuelson Theorem', in PETER MORRIS OPPEDHEIMER, ed., *Issues in International Economics*, Stockfields: Oriel Press, 1978, pp. 138-53.

CHARLES P. KINDLEBERGER

ECONOMIC LAWS
AND ECONOMIC HISTORY

The four *Raffaele Mattioli Lectures* were delivered by Charles P. Kindleberger at the Luigi Bocconi University in Milan, from 12th to 14th May 1980.

FIRST LECTURE
Engel's Law

1. Introduction. – 2. Engel's law and growth. – 3. Engel's law as a general law of consumption. – 4. The Gompertz curve and the law of transformation as generalizations of Engel's law. – 5. Limits of the generalizations of Engel's law as explanations of take-off stages in growth processes.

1. Introduction

Engel's law is the first of the explanatory models to be examined in these lectures. Needless to say, the Engel I have in mind is the statistician, Ernst, from Saxony, not the manufacturer-radical, Friedrich Engels of Barmen in the Ruhr; his law, derived from budget studies, states that as income grows, the consumption of food grows less than proportionately per capita. I propose to claim, not on the basis of budget studies, or of archival research, but rather of casual empiricism, that Engel's law is much more general, and intrinsically is related to the Gompertz or S-curve, or the law of material transformation. In its limited form, associated with food, it provides powerful insight into the course of economic history. Generalized, it requires economists and economic historians to be wary of relying upon what Rostow calls the "imperatives of geometric growth". Nothing grows geometrically at a steady rate for very long. Growth begins slowly, picks up speed, rockets along, and then slows down. Discontinuity is endemic, if only in the second derivative. The case of food will be discussed first.

NOTE: *Charles Kindleberger introduced his Lectures with the following remarks*: It is a great honour and pleasure for me to give one in the set of lectures in memory of Raffaele Mattioli. I had the good fortune to meet Dr Mattioli. In 1971 I was on a trip in Italy talking to economists about the outlook for the Italian economy in preparation for an essay that appeared in *Il Caso Italiano*, and learned that he wanted to see me. In a delightful half hour we spent discussing the state of the world, he told me he "collected" economists. It was flattering to be added to his collection, and a relief not to be pinned like a butterfly, or stuffed like a bird. I also often think of Dr Mattioli when I read the distinguished series of economic histories of Italy – the overall study by Gino Luzzatto, of which unhappily only one volume was completed, and the series of regional studies by so many outstanding economic historians. That collection has external economies for us all that make it a fitting monument by the Banca Commerciale Italiana and Dr Mattioli, to celebrate the centenary of Italian independence.

3

2. Engel's law and growth

Engel's law expressed diminishing returns in utility to consumption of food in the 132 Belgian families whose budgets had been gathered by LePlay. The law has the corollary that as productivity increases, resources must be shifted out of agriculture into manufacturing or services, in order to provide the appropriate balance in consumption. Poor countries maintain most of their labour, land and other factors in the production of food in agriculture. In underdeveloped countries there is difficulty in assigning the work of given factors completely to one or another sector, but as a rough approximation, the poorest countries have 80 to 85 per cent of their resources in agriculture, and with continued growth this proportion declines perhaps to as low as 3 per cent. What the lower limit will be depends on the country's position in foreign trade. If it is an exporter of food like the United States, New Zealand or Denmark, the proportion will be higher than if it imports food like the United Kingdom or Belgium. Provided there is growth in the productivity of factors, transformation out of agriculture is inexorable.

It was the Australians, Allan G.B. Fisher and Colin Clark, who proposed the designations of primary, secondary and tertiary sectors, and the laws, deriving from Engel's law, that with economic growth the primary sector shrinks, while the secondary sector (manufacturing and construction, plus, in some definitions, mining) and the tertiary sector (services, including commerce, transport, government and personal services) grow.[1]

When growth and Engel's law are combined with other possibilities in the economy, the explanatory richness of Engel's law increases. John Kenneth Galbraith, for example, has suggested that the owner of a scarce factor in a society tries to exercise a monopoly in it, obtaining rents in income, prestige and political power.[2] Thus, if the generalization is not too sweeping, ownership

1. COLIN CLARK, *The Conditions of Economic Progress*, New York: St. Martin's Press, 1940 (3rd edition, 1957); ALLAN G. B. FISHER, 'Economic Implications of Material Progress', *International Labour Review*, July 1935, pp. 5-18; and 'Production Primary, Secondary and Tertiary', *Economic Record*, vol. xv, No. 28, June 1939, pp. 24-38.
2. JOHN KENNETH GALBRAITH, *The New Industrial State*, Boston: Houghton Mifflin; London: Hamish Hamilton, 1967.

4

of good land is prized in a poor economy, and gives rise to an aristocracy. Note the limitation about good land. Where land is poor, and there is no surplus to be guarded, or appropriated by the aristocracy, political organization takes the form of a weak nobility, as for example in Norway, or even republics, as in the mountainous regions of Switzerland. (I have some difficulty in fitting Italy, Spain and Portugal, with poor land and powerful aristocracies into this generalization; these cases may be due to erosion which destroyed a once rich land, while the nobility retained power, or to other factors not taken into account in the present model). In an economy in which factors are leaving agriculture for commerce and industry, capital tends to be the scarce resource, with its owners asserting their right to rents, and to access to the seats of government. Bourgeois society is thus republican, or if monarchy is retained, it is a constitutional one. Somewhat narcissistically, Galbraith holds that in a post-industrial society brains are the scarce resource, the intelligentsia is entitled to claim big rewards, and the bureaucracy, both in business and government, is increasingly likely to obtain control over the course of affairs. Extend the analysis still further from Engel's law – and we are getting remote I shall admit – and we observe that success in commerce, banking and industry in many societies leads back to ownership of land, to country estates, and pride in improving agriculture. This is presumably a reflection of cultural lag, in which the bourgeois still ape the aristocrats after economic and political power has to a degree shifted into their hands. The merchant is the best of improvers, said Adam Smith in discussing farming, but as a rule this occurred only after the merchant had built a great house, or extended an old one, as a form of income-elastic conspicuous consumption.

If the reluctance of any group to yield political power is added to growth and Engel's law, one obtains the result that agriculture tends to be overrepresented in parliamentary governments. In the United States, this effect was initially thought to have been brought under control by the constitutional requirement that the House of Representatives be redistricted, and the seats redistributed, following each decennial census. The method of allocating seats within the separate states, after redistricting, however, was left to state legislatures, and these in turn suffered from political lag and overrepresentation of agricultural interests. Not until the Supreme Court decreed that state legislatures were constitutionally bound to give equal access to power to urban and rural voters, with one man, one vote, did the domination of farm interests come under control, and with it farm-representative seniority on Congressional committees. As a footnote of some interest, perhaps mainly to those with a detailed knowledge of American geography, James Phinney Baxter, the late historian in the Turner frontier tradition, reacted to these propositions by hypothesizing that one of the last acts of the farm sector when its power in state legislatures was slipping in the 19th century, was to transfer the capital of the state from the major urban centre to a modest city on the fall line, where the plains give way to hills. Thus in Maine, Portland yielded place to Augusta as the capital; in New Hampshire, Portsmouth to Concord; in New York, New York City to Albany; in Pennsylvania, Philadelphia to Harrisburg; in South Carolina, Charleston to Columbia; in Georgia, Milledgeville to Atlanta. There are exceptions to the rule, as in Massachusetts, where the capital stayed in Boston, so the generalization is unsafe for accurate predictions.

3. Engel's law as a general law of consumption

Engel's law applies to more than food, and by extension to agriculture. It is a general law of consumption. With growth, demand for some one or more products – but only a few at a time – starts off with high income elasticity, and then declines as income rises much more. Increasing returns in consumption are followed by stable and then diminishing returns. Often in a modern economy, there is some one or more items of consumption – automobile, television set, colour television, holiday cottage – which is very much sought after. In 1955, when I was teaching at Harvard Summer School, a Japanese sociologist confirmed this generalization about consumption patterns, and said that in Japan at that time, the crucial item of consumption was the mixmaster: an electric kitchen device for stirring and blending food. Conversations were dominated by discussion of the mixmaster: "Do you have one yet? How do you like yours? We hope to get one by the end of the year." It is ironic to think that in twenty-five years Japan's spectacular rise in income has left the mixmaster far behind.

A given item may go through the Engel's consumption cycle of a luxury, with high income elasticity, to a necessity with low elasticity, more than once. On the first time through, the society is relatively poor, and the item is critical to the level of living of the family, perhaps a bicycle in a family in Asia, a Topolino in an Italian household of the 1930s, a radio in Europe or the United States in the 1920s. In due course when the item has been fully incorporated in the standard of living of the average family as a necessity, with low income elasticity, it comes around again as an income-elastic luxury, but as a bicycle for a child, rather than for the wage-earner, or the second car, the second or third radio or television set. The income elasticity of demand in a multi-car family is different for each vehicle. A sort of product cycle applies to demand as well as to the supply side, as the taste for products is diffused, along with the production technology, and income rises.

At the bottom of the cycle the good may become an inferior one, with negative income elasticity, because consumption actually declines as income rises. The potato and cheap sausages are the classic examples, to which one can add the first bicycle when the household buys a car, or the Volkswagen Beetle before the family trades up to an Opel or Mercedes. Historically one could trace in France in the 18th and 19th centuries, a number of grades of woollen textiles, each of which started out when developed in being sold to the upper classes, and in Paris, and which were then diffused to the provinces, to all classes, and finally, replaced in the home market by superior goods that had been introduced, ending up exported to the West Indies for use by slaves.[1]

In consumer theory, some analysts contemplate a "bliss point" where demand for all goods and services is sated, and all income elasticities apart from replacements have sunk to zero on the average. There may be some positive income elasticities for quality goods, but these would be offset by negative elasticities for the inferior ones. Some very small parts of some societies may be approaching this point, but clearly no nations as a whole, and not the world. And even at the bliss point, an economic problem remains. Staffan Burenstam Linder observes in *The Harried Leisure Class*, that affluence, which Adam Smith used to call opulence, leaves the consumer too little time to consume his abundant goods and services.[2] The need will remain to economize time. From another point of view opulence for all, when private goods are readily acquired in copious quantities, will still leave problems of congestion – a public bad – and a scarcity of privacy, a private intangible good.

Having quoted him with approval earlier, I may quarrel with Galbraith now.[3] Diffusion of tastes for private goods takes place only partly through advertising. The distinction between goods that are necessary (called by Adam Smith those of "use of necessity") and those that are wasteful (Smith's "fashion and fancy")

---

1. See FRANÇOIS DORNIC, *L'industrie textile dans le Maine et ses débouches internationales (1630-1815)*, Le Mans: Editions Pierre-Belon, 1955, p. 40 and Chapter v; and PIERRE GOUBERT, *Familles marchands sous l'Ancien Régime: Danse et les Motte, de Beauvais*, Paris: S.E.V.P.E.N., 1959, p. 174.

2. STAFFAN BURENSTAM LINDER, *The Harried Leisure Class*, New York: Columbia University Press, 1970.

3. JOHN KENNETH GALBRAITH, *The New Industrial State, op. cit.*

is quite unacceptable.[1] Demand for all but a minimum of food, clothing and shelter at a primitive level is determined socially, or perhaps sociologically, by emulation of other consumers, a peer group chosen by some social process that economists are not required to understand. Advertising certainly plays a role in many of these, but demand spreads as fast for many goods that are not advertised – symphony music, art museums and the like, and for activities such as skiing, sailing, and more recently jogging, roller skating and disco music. David Riesman's *The Lonely Crowd* asserts not only that much of American society is outer-directed, deriving its notions of good and bad from the peer group it chooses to emulate, but also that inner-directed persons, who appear to be independent in their judgments and tastes, have derived their mind-sets at an early age and simply become fixed in their ways.[2] We teach in our classes consumer sovereignty and independent utility functions. In actuality the position is more nearly that the consumer is ruled by his peer group and his utility functions interact with those of his kind.

New products expand rapidly, spread widely to the extent that they become mass-consumed, and then must slow down in rate of growth. This is Engel's law in extension and means that the geometric growth for any product must slow down. Some years ago John Meyer ascribed the Climacteric in Britain's growth at the end of the 19th century to the failure of exports to continue their rapid expansion of the third quarter of the century.[3] But the income elasticity of demand for such products as cotton textiles, iron and steel rails, galvanized iron sheets, was bound to fall as the world demand became saturated. Part of the growth in cotton textiles had been the result of competition with hand-woven textiles – woollens, linen and cotton produced by cottage indus-

1. ADAM SMITH, *An Inquiry into the Nature and Causes of the Wealth of Nations*, two volumes, London: Printed for W. Strahan and T. Cadell, 1766. The edition quoted is the text edited by Edwin CANNAN and published by Methuen and Co., London: Fourth edition, 1935. (Book I, Chapter x, Section b, para. 42), pp. 114-5.

2. DAVID RIESMAN, *The Lonely Crowd. A Study of the Changing American Character*, New Haven: Yale University Press, 1950.

3. JOHN R. MEYER, 'An Input-Output Approach to Evaluating the Influence of Exports on British Industrial Production in the late 19th Century', *Explorations in Entrepreneurial History*, vol. VIII, October 1955, pp. 12-34.

tries – first at home and then abroad. British industrial growth ultimately shrank for two reasons: Engel's law requiring reallocation into new industries, combined with British incapacity to transform rapidly into the new industries of chemicals, electrical equipment, and automobiles, on the one hand, and the competition of other countries in the old goods on the other. This competitive effect was noted by Tyszynski in his critique of the studies of the Institut für Weltwirtschaft und Seeverkehr in the *Enquête Ausschuss* which laid primary emphasis in relative rates of growth of exports on income elasticities for various products, which were thought to be fixed and ubiquitous, whereas on our showing, income elasticities for a given product will differ depending upon the level of income of a given society, and the distribution of income within it.[1] Thus for a country, income elasticities for particular products will change over time on average as income changes, and in cross-section, a given product will have different income elasticities in given countries, regions, social classes and the like, depending upon tastes and the income of the group in question. Nurkse's demonstration effect and cheap and easy communication appear to lead to the convergence of tastes internationally. Differences in income remain.

The competitive effect just discussed is distinct of course from Engel's law, and linked rather to the diffusion of technology on the output side of the product cycle. But the two effects work in conjunction to speed up the aging process in economies. Old goods have low income elasticities in rich societies, and import substitution works in poorer countries where the demand is higher and more income elastic, to reduce the export prospects of the pioneers. To sustain growth, the old economies must move on to new goods, with high income elasticities and with technologies not yet in process of adoption in importing countries. The process is endless, for in due course, the technology of these new products

1. INSTITUT FÜR WELTWIRTSCHAFT UND SEEVERKEHR AN DER UNIVERSITÄT KIEL, *Der deutsche Aussenhandel unter der Einwirkung weltwirtschaftlicher Strukturwandlungen*, (vol. 20 of the *Ausschuss zur Untersuchung der Erzeugungs-und Absatzbedingungen der deutschen Wirtschaft*), Berlin: E. S. Mittler & Sohn, 1932, pp. 156-7; H. TYSZYNSKI, 'World Trade in Manufactured Commodities, 1899-1950', *Manchester School of Economic and Social Studies*, vol. XIX, No. 3, September 1951, pp. 272-304.

becomes diffused too, and import substitution takes place, sometimes to the degree that the pioneer imports the product from its old market.

Some counterpart to this loss of export markets in old goods for developed countries takes place in what has been called a raw-material product cycle, which enables developed countries to substitute for imports of primary products. Magee and Robins recognize three stages in such a pattern: the first boom stage of derived demand, a second when there is substitution in demand and development of competitive sources of supply, and a third, when research and development produce economies in the product's use and synthetic substitutes.[1] Raw materials, like finished goods that enter into consumption, thus have a tendency to follow a generalized Engel's law.

1. STEPHEN P. MAGEE and NORMAN I. ROBINS, 'The Raw Materias Product Cycle', in LAWRENCE B. KRAUSE and HUGH T. PATRICK, eds., *Mineral Resources in the Pacific Area*, San Francisco: Federal Reserve Bank of San Francisco, 1978, pp. 30-55; 'Comments', pp. 57-68.

4. The Gompertz curve and the law of transformation as generalizations of Engel's law

Having briefly examined Engel's law in consumption, we may turn to a still more general statement of Engel's insight applicable to production as well as consumption, namely the "S" or Gompertz curve. This suggests that economic processes start slowly, pick up speed when successful, grow rapidly, and then slow down.

In one formulation this is the law of material transformation, which has been succinctly put by my M.I.T. metallurgist colleague, Cyril Stanley Smith:

"These and hundreds more materials and uses grew symbiotically through history, in a manner analogous to the S-curve of a phase transformation of the materials themselves. There was a stage, invisible except in retrospect, wherein fluctuations from the *status quo*, involving only small localized distortion began to interact and consolidate into a new structure; this nucleus then grew in a more or less constant environment at an increasing rate because of the increasing interfacial opportunity, until finally its growth was slowed and stopped by depletion of material necessary for growth, or by growing counterpressure of other aspects of the environment. Any change in conditions (thermodynamic = social) may provide another opportunity for a new phase. We all know how the superimposition of many small sequential S-curves themselves add up to the giant S-curve of that new and larger structure we call civilization . . . Because at any one time there are many overlapping competing sub-systems at different stages of maturity but each continually changing the environment of the others, it is often hard to see what is going on. Moreover, nucleation must in principle be invisible, for the germs of the future take their validity only from and in a larger system that has yet to exist. They are at first indistinguishable from mere foolish fluctuations destined to be erased. They begin in opposition to their environment, but on reaching maturity they form the new environment by the balance of their multiple reactions. This change of scale, and interface with time, is the essence of history of anything whatever, material, intellectual or social."[1]

1. CYRIL STANLEY SMITH, 'Metallurgy as Human Experience'. The 1974 Distinguished Lectureship in Materials and Society, *Metallurgical Transactions*, vol. LXII, No. 4, April 1975, p. 605.

The metallurgist naturally finds limitations on the supply side, and in today's world of energy problems, as in Ricardo's time of diminishing returns to the application of labour and capital to land, we are acutely aware of this force making for slowdown. I would argue, however, that one of the reasons for the slowdown of a given economy is that it is locked into the production of goods that are reaching their limits in consumption at a time when the competitive effect means that any declining overall increase in consumption goes to other producers. Before turning to slowdown the early fast-growing segment of the Gompertz curve should be discussed first.

Some years ago, W. W. Rostow introduced the notion of "take-off" into the discussion of economic growth.[1] His stages of growth started with (i) preconditions, went on to (ii) take-off, then (iii) the drive to maturity, and a final stage – as far as his discussion went – of high-level mass consumption. The analysis was strongly criticized for the implication that a stage of take-off could be dated fairly precisely – ascribed in the case of Britain to the single year 1783 when exports to the newly independent United States rose sharply – and also for the implication that all Western economies – and possibly even the socialist – would follow the same stages in more or less uniform fashion. In some economies such as Argentina, he and his students found a "long delay", but for the most part he thought his law of growth as useful for prediction as Marx claimed the materialistic dialectic was.[2]

Alexander Gerschenkron differentiated his model of economic growth from that of Rostow by claiming that there was no unique set of preconditions, but that one precondition could substitute for another. In particular, he believed that banks and government could substitute for vigorous entrepreneurship if that were missing in a country which was starting the process of development. Ultimately he expanded the likelihood of substitutes among

1. WALT WHITMAN ROSTOW, *The Stages of Growth*, Cambridge: Cambridge University Press, 1960.

2. GUIDO DI TELLA, *The Economic History of Argentina, 1914-1933*, Dissertation, Massachusetts Institute of Technology, 1960; and MANUEL ZYMELMAN, *The Economic History of Argentina, 1933-1952*, Dissertation, Massachusetts Institute of Technology, 1958.

the antecedent conditions of development into a theory of "backwardness", in which he held that the more backward an economy was at the start of industrialization, the more it was necessary for industrial banks, and in still more primitive cases, government to provide the driving force.[1] He sought, not very successfully in my judgment, to differentiate his notion of discontinuity, sometimes called "the big spurt", from Rostow's take-off. But like Rostow who recognized the "big delay" in Argentina, Gerschenkron was obliged to allow for *An Economic Spurt That Failed* in the experience of Austria in the first decade of the twentieth century.[2]

1. ALEXANDER GERSCHENKRON, 'Economic Backwardness in Historical Perspective', in BERTHOLD FRANK HOSELITZ, ed., *The Progress of Underdeveloped Areas*, Chicago: University of Chicago Press, 1952, reprinted in ALEXANDER GERSCHENKRON, *Economic Backwardness in Historical Perspective. A Book of Essays*, Cambridge, Mass.: Harvard University Press, 1962, pp. 5-30.

2. ALEXANDER GERSCHENKRON, *An Economic Spurt That Failed. Four Lectures in Austrian History*. Princeton: Princeton University Press, 1977.

5. Limits of the generalizations of Engel's law as explanations of take-off stages in growth processes

The central point of this lecture is that Engel's law is valid, as are its generalizations in the Gompertz or S-curve, and the law of transformation, with their phases of preconditions and prerequisites, take-off and the big spurt, self-sustaining growth and the like, but that none of it is much good for prediction. Recognizable *ex post*, they are often difficult to detect when the process is under way, and useless *ex ante*. On the one hand, the prerequisites may not be recognizable until growth actually takes place. On the other, a series of S-curves or little take-offs in this and that industry may so pile on top of each other that the clean, clear shape of the overall S-curve is blurred and unrecognizable even at a distance.

For the first example, one can cite Sweden which has recently been called for the first half of the nineteenth century, the "impoverished sophisticate". This characterization is meant to suggest that it had all the preconditions of growth, with highly developed entrepreneurship, government, literacy, access to science, and the like, but no real path to development until the repeal of the Corn Laws, the timber duties and the Navigation Acts in the late 1840s opened up new markets for Swedish exploitation.[1] Swedish growth was rapid after about 1860, conforming to Rostovian stages, but until that time there was an abundance of prerequisites or preconditions, without much in the way of transformation and transforming growth.

On the second score, one can turn to the French experience in the first half of the nineteenth century. Rostow has spent a great deal of time dating "take-off" in various countries. As already noted, he has picked 1783 as the date for Britain, with the expansion of exports following the Treaty of Paris ending the War of Independence. The leading sector was cotton textiles. In France, take-off is said to have occurred from 1830 to 1860, with railroads as the leading sector. Recent research, however, has again raised

1. LARS G. SANDBERG, 'Banking and Economic Growth in Sweden before World War I', *Journal of Economic History*, vol. xxxviii, No. 3, September 1978, pp. 650-80.

a serious question whether there ever was an industrial *revolution* in France. Richard Roehl finds steady growth throughout the period from Waterloo to the Second Empire, which, one can hypothesize, is based on a series of small S-curves in one industry after another, none with the same timing, so that the overall curve is dampened. Canal-building, mining, textiles, railroads, sugar-refining, urban construction, one industry after another takes off more or less quietly, to a certain extent by itself. However, there is no sector that so dominates overall the average as to be called leading.[1] In Rostow's system there is some difficulty in determining whether a leading sector leads in size, rate of growth, rate of technological change, forward or backward linkages, or some combination of these elements with changing weight. Railroads started in France in the 1830s, but picked up speed in construction only after the financing problems were solved in the 1850s. When a country such as Canada has a series of sectors – furs, fishing, timber, mining, wheat, paper – that lead in speed of growth for a time and then slow down to a more measured pace, there may appear to be a series of take-offs, but little in the way of an overall take-off leading to sustained growth. Even in a single industry, little S-curves may grow out of earlier S-curves, as when an industry gets a new lease on life through innovation. The Gilchrist Thomas and Martin processes following Bessemer in steel provide an illustration.

The lesson to be drawn from this is that growth is not more, it is change. There are economists who make a distinction between growth, which is more, and development, which is transformation from one to another sector in weighting, from one technology to another, from one set of institutions to another. If one adopts this scheme, it implies that growth is a short-run phenomenon, for in the longer run growth and transformation must converge. The change does not have to take place in given actors. These may move off centre stage, and give way to a new set who can perform the different tasks. In fact, it seems to be close to an economic law that change requires a new cast, since the old set

1. RICHARD ROEHL, 'French Industrialization: A Reconsideration', *Explorations in Economic History*, vol. XIII, No. 3, July 1976, pp. 233-81.

are unable to turn their minds effectively to new tasks. But growth cannot mean more of the same, because Engel's law means that the world will not continue to want more, in the same way. And the competitive effect means that even the same amount, assuming that the range of inferior goods is limited, will tend to be produced by someone else, who is willing, after acquiring the technique, to do it more cheaply.

Geometric growth is a will-o'-the-wisp. Babies who double their birthweight in five months and triple it in a year end up weighing a finite number of kilograms. Trees never reach the sky. If the woods are growing, it is necessary to have new trees, and not to stick to the old ones. Geometric growth, and log-scale charts illuminate a number of problems, but are not helpful in economic history. They are wrong after all but a limited burst of expansion in a single industry. While one can fit a growth trend to an S-curve, it has little or no predictive value. And when one turns to aggregating industries, the index-number problem raises its head.

The work of Gerschenkron on production indexes in Italy and the Soviet Union is well known.[1] Choice between a Laspeyres and a Paasche index makes wide differences in calculated rates of growth because of the difference in weighting. In particular, the Soviet Union seriously overstated its rate of growth by using base-year weights, when new and rapidly growing goods were scarce, hence high-priced, and hence overweighted. End-year weights, on the other hand, understate rates of growth, and chained indexes with changing weights achieve an uneasy compromise. National-income statistics, of course, are subject to the same index-number problems, albeit in a dampened form because of the hundreds or thousands of items included. It is difficult to have confidence in rates of growth of individual countries over periods as long as 50 to 100 years. When two countries are compared, as in the book by O'Brien and Keyder on France and Britain, the result is not likely to attract instant complete confidence. In addition to the index-number problems in the separate countries, which may have different biases, the

---

1. ALEXANDER GERSCHENKRON, 'Economic Backwardness in Historical Perspective', *op. cit.*, Chapters 4, 9, 10.

difficulty of cross-section analysis makes it virtually impossible to find a trustworthy base for starting, ending, or pinning down the middle years. The O'Brien-Keyder finding that France in 1789 was richer per capita than Britain strikes me as incredible in the light of Engel's law and the fact, or rather the estimate, that British agriculture at that time employed 57 per cent of the labour force, and French agriculture 81 per cent.[1]

I return to the need to transform with growth, that is, to shift resources out of existing industries into new ones as growth proceeds, or to direct the flow of labour out of agriculture into industry and services as output per capita grows with savings, education, and improved technology. The idea is hardly new. In writing on *The Terms of Trade* a quarter century ago, I concluded that the terms of trade changed not against primary products and in favour of manufactures, but in favour of developed countries and against developing countries (as they are euphemistically called) which is not the same thing.[2] The reason was that developed countries, as I then thought, had the capacity to transform, and poor countries, less developed countries, or primary producers did not. When prices of goods that primary producers exported rose, new entry in other less developed countries and in the developed countries brought them down again. When such prices fell, inability of the primary producers to achieve exit from their export lines meant that those prices stayed down, relative to those of manufactured exports. If price changes are stochastically distributed, primary-producing countries that face new entry when prices rise, and are unable to exit when prices fall, will experience a long-run declining trend in terms of trade. For developed countries at their prime, the position was the reverse; increases in prices could be sustained, because new entry was difficult, and price declines were met by effective exit, which brought them up again.

1. PATRICK O'BRIEN and CAGLAR KEYDER, *Economic Growth in Britain and France, 1780-1914. Two Paths to the Twentieth Century*, London: George Allen & Unwin, 1978, calculated from table 4.5, p. 94.

2. CHARLES P. KINDLEBERGER, *The Terms of Trade: A European Case Study* (with the assistance of Hermann G. VAN DER TAK and Jaroslav VANEK), Cambridge, Mass.: Technology Press; New York: John Wiley and Sons; London: Chapman & Hall, 1956.

This was the position as I judged it in 1955. Today I would take a different view. The Rostovian stages of growth ending in an endless period of high mass consumption seem rather like the fairy tales in which the Prince marries the maiden and they live happily ever afterward. At the top of the Gompertz curve, however, a country does not experience continued growth in the production of mass consumption goods but a loss in capacity to transform, in ability to respond to price signals, to get out of old industries with the low income elasticities, and to enter new ones (or to employ new processes coming to the fore in old industries). Britain had no place to go at the turn of this century in cotton textiles, coal, iron and steel rails, tinplate, galvanized iron sheets, and the like, and found it difficult to effect new entry into electrical equipment, chemicals and automobiles. I should note that this is a controversial judgment on which the last word has not been said. After years of leading the world in exports of airplanes, computers, electronic equipment, the United States is faced in the long run with the necessity to exit from these industries as technological diffusion continues its inexorable way, with no clear direction in which to go. In the United States the rate of innovation has declined, as have the rate of investment and that of productivity increase. Like Britain in the last third of the nineteenth century, the United States is an aging economy, slowly losing its capacity to transform. The competitive effect in turn continues to press. Some years ago I said ironically that the United States' most dynamic product was soya-beans. After the sharp run-up in price in 1973, when President Nixon shocked the Japanese by imposing an embargo on soya-bean exports, it turns out that Brazil has suddenly moved into soya-bean production at a faster rate than the United States. A sad illustration of inability to adapt and transform is provided by the sorrowful record of United States' failure thus far to adapt to the OPEC rise in oil prices, either in finding and producing more oil, developing substitutes, or cutting back consumption through conservation or an elastic response of demand. Mexico, with its new finds and despite its Gulf spill, and Canada, reacted in more youthful and transforming ways.

Thus, it can be accepted that Engel's law with its generalization from food to consumption as a whole, and from consumption to the Gompertz or S-curve, is a tool that belongs in the economic historian's kit. There are those, braver than I, who would use it in forecasting. In Daniel Bell's *The Coming of Post-Industrial Society*, continued increases in output, perhaps accelerated by computerized factories, encounter decreasing returns in consumption of goods and will divert resources increasingly into services, which remain income-elastic.[1] The guess is a good one, but it remains a guess. History offers examples of "failed transitions", and of straightforward declines.[2] With many forces at work and small changes in the scale of any one capable of producing an overall difference in trend, it is tempting the gods to forecast even a short distance ahead as is amply demonstrated by Colin Clark's *The Economics of 1960* written in 1942, or the Brookings Institution's *The Balance of Payments of the United States in 1968* written in 1963.[3] I urge the usefulness of Engel's law in interpreting history, but am as yet unwilling to lean heavily on it in peering into the future.

1. DANIEL BELL, *The Coming of Post-Industrial Society: A Venture in Social Forecasting*, New York: Basic Books; London: Heinemann, 1973.

2. FREDERICK KRANTZ and PAUL M. HOHENBERG, *Failed Transitions to Modern Industrial Society: Renaissance Italy and Seventeenth Century Holland*, Montreal: Inter-university Center for European Studies, 1975.

3. COLIN CLARK, *The Economics of 1960*, London: Macmillan, 1942; WALTER S. SALANT *et al.*, *The Balance of Payments of the United States in 1968*, Washington, D.C.: Brookings Institution, 1963.

SECOND LECTURE
The Iron Law of Wages

1. The Lewis growth model. – 2. An application to Western Europe. – 3. The Lewis model and United States' growth. – 4. Lewis model and "Europe's Post-war Growth". – 5. The case when there is no exogenous source of growth.

1. The Lewis growth model

The first lecture dealt with Engel's law that holds that agricultural output grows more slowly than the economy as a whole because of diminishing returns to and capacity for consumption in food. An important corollary, of great explanatory significance for much economic history, is that as industry and services grow, and if productivity in agriculture grows as well, a supply of labour becomes available in agriculture for transfer to the other sectors. If one adds population growth in agriculture and an excess of workers attached to agriculture, we can readily arrive at the W. Arthur Lewis model of "growth with unlimited supplies of labour".[1] It has a strong family resemblance to Karl Marx's model of growth that exploits an industrial reserve army. The title of this lecture is perhaps a misnomer, as the iron law of wages of, say, Ricardo or Malthus holds in the longer period than that in which I am interested, when it holds at all, and runs to the effect that wages cannot rise above the subsistence level because if they were to do so, population would expand to bring them down again. The Lewis or the Marxian model of growth with an elastic supply of labour to draw upon is akin to the iron law of wages insofar as it assumes that wages are fixed at some subsistence level, which may in fact rise gradually over time as the concept of the subsistence level of living inches up because of Duesenberry effects, but the emphasis is different. The Lewis model is interested in growth, and posits an elastic supply of labour in the short run available at the subsistence wage; the iron law of

1. WILLIAM ARTHUR LEWIS, 'Economic Development with Unlimited Supplies of Labour', *Manchester School of Economic and Social Studies.* vol. XXII, No. 2, May 1954, pp. 139-91.

wages is interested in income distribution, and assumes not a standing army of unemployed or underemployed labourers in agriculture, but the mechanism of demographic change. I may be guilty of misrepresentation in choosing this title for symmetry among the four lecture titles.

As in the discussion of Engel's law, we are required to assume a source of economic growth from outside the system – a discovery, innovation, a positive shift in the demand for an exported product, or the like. This raises the marginal efficiency of labour in the secondary sector, let us say, and makes possible an expansion of output. If there is a reserve army of unemployed, or unemployed and underemployed on the farm waiting for an opportunity to come to the city at the existing wage, output will expand without raising wages, profits and rents will increase, making possible increased savings in the industrial sector, and reinvestment which in turn raises once again the marginal efficiency of labour. So long as more labour is available at constant wages, without strongly diminishing returns to other factors such as management or land, a positive feedback process is under way. Growth in the industrial sector continues to lead to growth in the industrial sector.

The position of the agricultural sector is also helped. It is assumed that labour on the farm is paid an average farm wage (about half that in the industrial sector according to Colin Clark's law), but that it produces at the margin less than the wage, perhaps zero (or perhaps even a negative amount because the last workers get in the way of the others), but in any event less than the going wage.[1] Farmers tolerate the situation of workers paid more than their marginal product, because these are typically members of the family, or of the community. The excess that they are paid over what they earn in economic terms comes out of the share of land, which would otherwise be paid as rent. On this account, the loss of workers to the industrial sector increases income per capita of those on the farm, and increases the return to the owner of the land. Income per capita rises both in in-

---

[1]. COLIN CLARK, *The Conditions of Economic Progress*, New York: St. Martin's Press, 1940; Third edition, 1957, Chapter IX.

dustry and agriculture, as profits in industry and rents in agriculture are increased. Agriculture, like industry, is in a better position to save. If agricultural savings are invested in industry, as Fei and Ranis have thought in their exegesis of the Lewis model, the industrial sector is furnished the wherewithal to buy food to feed the new workers.[1] Or the savings may be reinvested in agriculture: in machines bought from industry, which requires marketing the food in the city, too, or in kind, such as draining, fencing, building herds and flocks, and the like, which poses a problem of feeding the newly-recruited industrial workers in the short run, but contributes to agricultural productivity over the long. Increases in agricultural productivity, simultaneously with or consequent to the initial outside stimulus in the industrial sector, will add to the number of workers who can be diverted from agriculture to industry, and sustain the virtuous, or positive, feedback process.

When the availability of labour for the industrial sector runs out, the nature of the growth process changes drastically. An increase in the marginal efficiency of labour leads not to expanded output at the old wage, but to higher wages; not to increased property incomes available for reinvestment, but to unchanged, or possibly reduced, property incomes and a decline in the investment rate. Real incomes of workers rise, and with them the demand for consumption goods. Investment slows down in response to higher wages and unchanged or reduced profits – called by Marxists surplus value. Marxists foresee a crisis of overproduction and declining profits; they seem not to give much attention to the rise in the real income of workers.

1. JOHN C. H. FEI and GUSTAV RANIS, *Development of the Labor Surplus Economy. Theory and Policy*, Homewood, Ill.: Irwin, 1964.

2. An application to Western Europe

I first applied the Lewis model to Western European growth after World War II.[1] Unlimited supplies of labour were available to the industrial sector in Western Europe from various sources: pre-war unemployed, German expellees and refugees from Eastern Europe; from agriculture; from the artisanry; from normal growth of population which, prior to the war in such countries as the Netherlands, had been emigrating; and as the 1950s progressed and merged into the 1960s, from the Mediterranean countries and regions. This labour supply, originally thought to be a burden, proved to be a blessing. It sustained what I called "supergrowth" for almost two decades after the end of the war. This interesting case will be examined later. First I propose to examine the role of unlimited supplies of labour in the industrial revolution in Britain. The subject is not uncontroversial. Such an astute observer as Sidney Pollard has grave doubts that the Lewis model applies to the industrial revolution, maintaining that the increase in industrial labour came from the natural increase in population in the countryside, not from unemployed or underemployed farm workers.[2] An observer of a century ago, Walter Bagehot, thought that labour did not migrate: "Man," he contended, "is of all pieces of luggage the most difficult to be removed".[3] Elsewhere he conceded that capital and labour were readily mobile from occupation to occupation and place to place in England in the 1870s, but believed that in most ages and most countries, the tendency of labour and capital to move easily had been defeated by xenophobia keeping invaders out, by slavery, ineffective government, or the needs of a national defence that depended on localized persons.[4]

1. Charles P. Kindleberger, *Europe's Postwar Growth: The Role of the Labor Supply*, Cambridge, Mass.: Harvard University Press; London: Oxford University Press, 1967.
2. Sidney Pollard, 'Labour in Great Britain', in Peter Mathias and Moisei Mikhail Postan, eds., *The Cambridge Economic History of Europe*, vol. vii, *The Industrial Economies: Capital, Labour, and Enterprise*, Part 1: *Britain, France, Germany, and Scandinavia*, Cambridge: Cambridge University Press, 1978, pp. 107-8.
3. Walter Bagehot, 'Adam Smith and Our Modern Economy', in *Economic Studies*, edited by Richard Holt Hutton, London: Longmans. First edition 1880, Second edition 1888; reprinted in *The Collected Works of Walter Bagehot*, edited by Norman St John-Stevas, vol. xi, London: The Economist, 1978, pp. 298-328; see p. 313.
4. Walter Bagehot, 'The Postulates of English Political Economy. No. 1', *Fortnightly Review*, No. cx, N. S., 1st February, 1876, pp. 215-42; reprinted in *The Collected Works of Walter Bagehot, op. cit.*, vol. xi, pp. 222-54; see pp. 222 ff.

Despite these caveats, I believe that the Lewis model fits the facts of the British industrial revolution quite well. Industrial growth took place in the Midlands and in the north, pulling additions to the farm population into the city. The major centre of increased agricultural productivity was in Norfolk and East Anglia, and further south in Kent and Sussex, based on new techniques imported from Holland. Labour in this area was drawn not so much into industry, as into London service occupations on the one hand, and into transatlantic migration on the other. Increased capital investment took place in the north and Midlands both from ploughed back profits and from agricultural incomes, relayed from the southeast to the northwest through London banks. One extraneous force was the Speenhamland system of work relief, adopted in 1795, which subsidized agricultural wages and hence lowered the wage level.[1] This was the unintended result of a measure taken to prevent agricultural vagrants from wandering from parish to parish in search of relief, and to ensure that they be taken care of where they resided. That unhappy system was scrapped with the Poor Law of 1832.

It is ironic that Friedrich Engels went from Barmen in the Rhineland to Manchester to study the textile industry a decade before the time that the rapidly growing economy of Lancashire was encountering labour shortages. When he was there, wages were abysmally low, housing appalling, workers drowned their misery in drink.[2] The 1840s were also "hungry" because of industrial depression and short crops. It was a poor time to get a reading on the potential of the system, and Engels, like many continental observers of less radical persuasion, was deeply moved. Just ahead, however, was a change in prospect. In the 1850s, after the fiscal reform which rationalized the system of customs duties, followed by repeals of the Corn Laws, the Navigation Acts and the timber duties, there was a rise in output, wages, and the level of living, conforming to the Lewis model when the elastic supply of labour became exhausted and the labour

1. KARL POLANYI, *The Great Transformation*, New York: Farrar and Rinehart, 1944.
2. FRIEDRICH ENGELS, *The Condition of the English Working Classes in 1848*, London: Allen & Unwin, 1892, see Chapter 5.

supply was limited. The Hungry 'Forties were followed by the Golden Age of Farming, despite the repeal of the Corn Laws and substantial increases in imports of breadstuffs from East Prussia, and meat and dairy products from Holland and increasingly from Denmark. The system was one which is scornfully known today as "trickledown", with the level of living rising first for the upper and middle classes, then for farmers, and only slowly for industrial workers. Rise it nonetheless did, especially after 1875 for those who retained their employment during the Great Depression. Profits were then falling – indeed, the period is sometimes characterized as less a Great Depression than as profitless prosperity – and real wages were rising.

The Lewis model worked in the intermediate run. The iron law of wages failed to hold over the longer period as population growth did not keep up with the rise in real income. The death rate fell – changes in medicine, relatively unimportant in the eighteenth century, may have begun to take effect in the mid-nineteenth, and gradually the noisome cities were provided with improved drainage, fewer rats, and the urban worker with cheaper clothing, more readily kept clean. But the birth rate declined too in a Malthusian counter-revolution that rendered the iron law obsolete.

Population pressure in peasant agriculture may build up before the factory stage is reached in industrialization, and produce what Franklin Mendels has called proto-industrialization, or large-scale cottage industry.[1] In Britain, this resulted in handloom weavers and hand nailers, who survived in considerable agony because of factory competition, down to the middle of the nineteenth century. On the Continent, it was extended to many other industries, including cotton and wool spinning, along with weaving, and in Switzerland watchmaking. A Swiss sociologist, Rudolf Braun, writing on the Züricher Oberland, insists that the cotton-textile industry, with home spinning and weaving, and merchants who brought the raw materials to the cottage and marketed the finished product, strongly favoured the preservation

1. FRANKLIN F. MENDELS, 'Proto-Industrialization: The First Phase of the Process of Industrialization', *Journal of Economic History*, vol. xxx, No. 1, March 1972, pp. 241-61.

of the family. The alternative to cottage industry, given the pressure of population on the land, was "wandering", the restless search for work either in the dead season, or on a permanent, year-round basis. With proto-industrialization, agriculture first provided labour for cottage industry; in a second stage, cottage industry provided workers for the more efficient factories. One of many tragedies in such a system was that the best hand spinners were the longest to hold out against the factory. "The strong swimmers perish more slowly."[1]

The Lewis model applied to Britain, I would claim, and to Switzerland. Something akin to it has been used by Joel Mokyr to explain why Belgium industrialized in the 19th century and the Netherlands did not. Labour was cheap in Belgium, expensive in the Netherlands.[2] The cheapness of Belgian labour is explained like that of Switzerland, by the availability of an unlimited supply, maintained in a holding pattern by proto-industrialization and population pressure. Thousands of cottage workers were crowded into a narrow geographical space. In the Netherlands, labour was expensive for a peculiar reason, if Mokyr is correct, and one which is a variant on the iron law of wages. The cost of living was high because taxes had been levied on consumption, rather than on trade. The Dutch stapling trade thrived on buying and selling, importing and re-exporting, and the Dutch mercantile oligopoly wanted no taxes on goods that would in any way inhibit their importing, finishing, repackaging and shipping for staple commodities. Low transit duties were accepted for goods that were sent through Amsterdam without charge, but a system of tariffs and drawbacks, under which duties paid were refunded when the goods were subsequently exported, was thought to be burdensome in the trouble it occasioned. Holland with a large public debt and a big navy to protect her colonial empire levied taxes on items of personal consumption, such as milling wheat and beer. This, together with the generous system of unemployment relief, made wages high, and likely to rise with any ex-

1. RUDOLF BRAUN, *Sozialer und kultureller Wandel in einem ländlichen Industriegebiet,* Erlenbach-Zurich: Eugen Rentsch, 1965.
2. JOEL MOKYR, *Industrialization in the Low Countries, 1795-1850,* New Haven: Yale University Press, 1976.

pansion of industry.[1] This system inhibited manufacturing more than did the thin supply of coal.

If the Dutch case illustrates the negative side of the Lewis model, the same is claimed, not without debate, for France. The early suggestion that equal inheritance of peasant farmland after the French Revolution sharply reduced population growth in the farm sector, as contrasted with primogeniture under which the first son inherited the entire property, in effect before 1789, is no longer readily accepted. Equal inheritance may make for small families, but it encourages early marriage, as each child is assured of access to some land, whereas primogeniture makes for bigger families but delays the age of marriage.[2] Moreover, rates of population growth were declining in France as early as 1780, before the change in system occurred, and declined much more sharply than over the Revolutionary and First Empire period during the 1846-1853 period of crop failures, revolution, low agricultural incomes and high rents. In addition, workers poured off the farms in two periods of rapid economic growth – the 1850s and the 1950s – and there was always a considerable seasonal movement between agriculture and industry, especially the Paris construction industry, as exemplified by the masons of Limousin.

Seasonal job-seeking is a compromise between the Lewis model and its opposite, clinging to the farm by land-hungry peasants. It is found widely in Europe from the Greeks who desert the villages for the cities after the harvest until the next planting,[3] to the Italian seasonal farm workers who moved north with the harvest, or even crossed the Atlantic to Argentina as *"golodrinos"* or swallows, to work the harvest there in the Italian winter. Nearly a million workers from Poland and the East who came to Germany to help with the harvest made possible the full-time relocation of German workers from East German agriculture to Silesian, Berlin and Ruhr industry before World War I.[4] Where

---

1. JOEL MOKYR, *Industrialization in the Low Countries, 1795-1850, op. cit.*, pp. 191-2.

2. Hrothgar JOHN HABAKKUK, 'Family Structure and Economic Change in Nineteenth Century Europe', *Journal of Economic History*, vol. xv, No. 1, March 1955, pp. 1-12.

3. WILLIAM HARDY McNEILL, *Greece: American Aid in Action, 1947-1956*, New York: Twentieth Century Fund, 1957, pp. 5-7.

4. GERD HARDACH, *The First World War, 1914-1918*, Berkeley: University of California Press, 1977, p. 110.

seasonal workers are not available to help with the harvest, there is strong pressure to bring recent emigrants to industry back to the farm from industry in summer. This imposes a seasonal strain on industry in early stages of industrialization. Olga Crisp notes in her study of Russian labour that some factories in that country followed a practice of raising wages in summer to limit the numbers of workers who would return to their homes to help with the harvest.[1]

Whether the Lewis model applies to a given country or not, and in what degree, is an appropriate subject of historical research and, in some instances, debate, as the French case, Pollard's question about Britain, and Mokyr's conclusions about Belgium and the Netherlands indicate. Volume VII of *The Cambridge Economic History of Europe* is organized to discuss Capital, Labour and Enterprise, and most of the treatment of labour raises this issue explicitly. In addition to Pollard who denies the applicability of the model to England, Crisp says it does not apply to Russia, and Taira regards it as inapplicable to Japan.[2] In the latter two cases, attachment to the soil and limited improvements in agricultural efficiency made recruitment of labour for industry a difficult and painful process, as it was not in Britain. In Japan, use was made especially of target workers, young women recruited for limited periods of time, between perhaps 17 and 24 years of age, who sought to work and save in order to earn a marriage portion. This model of recruitment of labour was also practised in the nineteenth century at a locale far removed in culture from Japan – at Lowell, Massachusetts – where young farm girls, kept in protected dormitories to limit their contact with the industrial world, worked to earn the several hundred dollars needed to marry well in the 1830s, back on the farm.[3] Today in South

1. OLGA CRISP, 'Labour and Industrialization in Russia', in PETER MATHIAS and MOISEI M. POSTAN, eds., *The Cambridge Economic History of Europe*, vol. VII, *The Industrial Economies: Capital, Labour, and Enterprise*, Part 2, *The United States, Japan, and Russia, op. cit.*, pp. 379, 386.

2. KOJI TAIRA, 'Factory Labour and the Industrial Revolution in Japan', in PETER MATHIAS and MOISEI M. POSTAN, eds., *The Cambridge Economic History of Europe, op. cit.*, Part 2, p. 169.

3. MICHEL CHEVALIER, *Lettres sur l'Amérique du Nord*, Third edition, Paris: Gosselin, 1838, vol. I, Lettre XIII, pp. 207-8.

Korea, Taiwan and Singapore, in textile mills, the same target work, resulting in a backward-bending supply curve of labour, brings young unmarried women effectively if briefly into the labour force of textile mills.[1]

The effect of an infinitely elastic supply of a given factor of production in sustaining growth, once the demand for increased inputs has been provided outside the system, is not confined to labour. In the northern United States, growth started and continued for most of the nineteenth century with unlimited supplies of land. Unlimited supply meant that land commanded no rent, and rents were earned by labour, itself in short supply, which was always free to move to the frontier and start farming if it did not like the wages or conditions of work in commerce or industry. "The West was always there to give refuge to unemployed arms."[2] From almost the beginning, Americans were "people of plenty" in David Potter's phrase.[3] Habakkuk claimed that in the United States innovation sought to save the scarce factor, labour, while innovation in Britain concentrated on saving resources, and especially energy.[4] This insight is intuitively attractive but confronts the analytical point that in equilibrium the marginal cost of an additional unit of output must be the same whether achieved through adding land, labour, capital, or enterprise. Relative scarcities cannot be calculated in a closed economy, but only in comparison with some other economy of no relevance to innovators. But of course if the economy is growing and different inputs have different elasticities of supply with respect to output, the point makes excellent sense. It is important to focus innovation on the input with the lowest supply elasticity for increases in output.

1. HENRY Y. WAN, 'Manpower, Industrialization and Export-led Growth – The Taiwan Experience', in YUAN-LI and KUNG-CHIA YEH, eds., 'Growth, Distribution and Social Change, Essays on the Economy of the Republic of China', *Occasional Papers / Reprints Series in Contemporary Asian Studies*, vol. xv, No. 3, 1978, published by the School of Law, University of Maryland, pp. 161-91, see pp. 167-79.

2. MICHEL CHEVALIER, *Lettres sur l'Amérique du Nord*, *op. cit.*, vol. i, p. 218.

3. DAVID M. POTTER, *People of Plenty: Economic Abundance and the American Character*, Charles R. Walgreen Foundation Lectures, Chicago: University of Chicago Press, 1954.

4. HROTHGAR JOHN HABAKKUK, *American and British Technology in the Nineteenth Century. The Search for Labour-Saving Inventions*, Cambridge: Cambridge University Press, 1962.

3. The Lewis model and United States' growth

The model of growth with unlimited supplies of land is relevant to wheat growing in the United States, less so to cotton, where slavery was needed to provide the large amount of labour needed with land. A radical view is that such slavery was competitive with labour in the North, holding down wages, so that northern labour too was subject to the iron law of wages and to the capitalist exploitation of surplus value. Mainstream analysts would not accept this view of the early position in the northern United States. Be that as it may, in due course the railroads penetrated the West, and settlement of veterans of the Civil War there with 40 acres and a mule meant that land was no longer free and no longer unable to command rent. It is perhaps no accident that Henry George's theory of the single tax on the rent of land was developed about this time as rents in the East were beginning to rise with the exhaustion of free land in the West.

But then came massive migration to the United States on a scale far in excess of the early British, mid-century Irish and German waves. The United States benefited first from free land, then from labour-saving innovation, and finally from the Lewis model of growth with unlimited supplies of labour. Many immigrants were target workers of the life-cycle variety, as opposed to those saving to buy a particular object – a husband, a fishing boat, some land, or the stock to start a store. They would come to the United States intending to work and stay for a generation, and then return to Greece, or Italy, or wherever, to retire and die. The net migratory movement was substantially less than the gross flow because of the gradually rising return flow, especially in the years from 1900 to 1913. Certainly, as in the European northward migration of the 1950s and 1960s, it was never clear in advance what form the pattern would take. The distinction between a temporary exit permit and a permanent one in the 1950s was arbitrary and meaningless from the point of view of the sending state, since the migrant retained his options and only time told what his behaviour would be. In the case of the United States, however, the possibilities of staying were substantial, at least until after World War I. The United States had a tradition of asylum, as did the Netherlands, for refugees from religious and political persecution. A simple and quick path to American citizenship meant that political bosses in the cities found it worthwhile to intermediate for immigrants and help them solve their problems, since they soon would be voters.

None of this, of course, applied to the blacks who were brought to the United States from Africa as slaves, against their will. I am afraid I lack any special insight into the economics of slavery, beyond noting the theory of my colleague Evsey Domar, that slavery and serfdom were a device to restrain mobility, to keep labour on the land when its loss would have raised wages and harmed agricultural production,[1] a view which finds echoes in Bagehot's analysis[2] of mobility and slavery a century ago.[3] However, it may be noted that emancipation during the Civil War did not lead to much migration of blacks until World Wars I and II, under the pressure of high demands for labour in the North, and that attempts to right ancient wrongs have led to social disturbances that seem, unhappily, not yet to be at an end.

Cultural and economic resistance to overseas immigration into the United States began fairly early in the 1880s, with limitations of the inflow of Asian peoples, and then of contract labour. The cultural resistance to immigration of Caucasians foundered against the obstacle of the 250-year-old tradition of asylum. A Boston middle-class movement sought to limit immigration, perhaps mainly of the Irish, through literacy tests. It failed. Only after World War I, when a large backlog of would-be immigrants had been built up in Europe that threatened to overwhelm the capacity of the country to assimilate foreign cultures into the

1. Evsey D. Domar, 'The Causes of Slavery or Serfdom: A Hyphothesis', *Journal of Economic History*, vol. xxx, No. 1, March 1970, pp. 18-32.

2. Walter Bagehot, 'The Postulates of English Political Economy. No. 1' *Fortnightly Review*, *op. cit.*; reprinted, in *The Collected Works of Walter Bagehot*, *op. cit.*, vol. xi, pp. 222-54, see pp. 251-4.

3. Reference should be made to the debate in the United States over the productivity of slaves in the production of cotton; see Robert W. Fogel and Stanley L. Engerman, *Time on the Cross*, voll. i and ii, Boston: Little, Brown, 1974; and the literature cited in Fogel and Engerman, 'Explaining the Relative Efficiency of Slave Agriculture in the Antebellum South, Reply', *American Economic Review*, vol. 70, No. 4, September 1980, pp. 672-90.

dominant English tradition, was limitation imposed, and then in such a way as to preserve the early pattern of British, German and Scandinavian origins of U.S. settlers. Perhaps an element in the restriction was the fear of labour which had gained in organized strength during the war that their wage structure would be undermined by unlimited immigration, along the lines of the Lewis model. In my historical judgment the restrictions were imposed primarily for social reasons related to the difficulties of acculturating large numbers. It is a problem that the country now faces with the vast numbers of Puerto Ricans, Mexicans and other Spanish-speakers in the country, legally or otherwise.

Migration is a social process in which economic and social elements do not always converge. Social forces can be redefined, of course, à la Gary Becker, to express them in economic terms, converting concern for culture and kinsfolk into costs of obtaining information or of overcoming ignorance. Migrants tend to move not solely where they can earn the highest monetary return, but follow family, villagers, compatriots, and settle where they can comfortably fit with their kind, even at some cost in wages. America, it has been demonstrated, was not a melting pot, as the myth had it, but a mosaic of foreign groups and clusters. When these became so large as to threaten the dominant culture with the possibility that in the second generation they would not conform to American standards, the gains to the United States from immigration with low wages, high profits and high rates of growth gave way to resistance to further migrants.

4. Lewis model and "Europe's Postwar Growth"

Much the same pattern seems to me to have expressed itself in Europe in the period after the Second World War, with economic and politico-socio-cultural patterns intertwined in a complex pattern. In 1967 in *Europe's Postwar Growth: The Role of the Labor Supply*, I advanced the notion that the Lewis model of growth with unlimited supplies of labour constituted a powerful analytical tool to help explain differential rates of growth between and among European countries.[1] Part of Britain's slow growth was owed to its reluctance to admit immigrant labour. The "stop-go" pattern under which each period of Keynesian expansion was rapidly brought to a halt by rising wages and a spillover of income into imports and a balance-of-payments deficit was a consequence of limited supplies of labour, and the reluctance, or rather unwillingness, of the trade unions to permit the entry of others from abroad. In the early days after the war, first displaced Poles and later Italian workers were sought by various industries, including especially the coal mines, but their admission was vetoed by the politically powerful trade unions. This resistance may well have had strictly economic roots. Later when the subjects to the Crown from the Commonwealth countries, who were entitled by their nationality to admission into the United Kingdom, began to come in increasing numbers from India, Pakistan, the British West Indies, and especially from Africa, although largely transplanted Indians and Pakistanis, the British government felt obliged for socio-cultural reasons to break the implicit contract involved in a common citizenship and common sovereignty, and to limit entry into the British Isles to those who already had arranged for a job. Since it was virtually impossible to find a job in Britain when one is outside the country, this halted the flow.

In Scandinavia and the Netherlands, cultural resistance first limited the flow to the Scandinavian Common Market for labour, in the case of Sweden, and to neighbouring Belgium and Luxembourg in the case of the Netherlands, until the virtual exhaustion of the labour supply and the need to resist inflation from the tide

1. See footnote 1, p. 24.

of rising wages overcame the hesitation and permitted immigration from the South. In Switzerland and West Germany, the order was reversed, with first a hearty welcome to foreign labour to discharge certain tasks that domestic workers were increasingly unwilling to accept, followed later by some socio-cultural concern, and the erection of barriers to continued immigration. In Switzerland, the limits on new entry were built almost exclusively on social grounds: one third of the labour force was foreign. This was viewed as a threat to the integrity of the Swiss nation, even though that was already a polyglot state. Economic arguments could be adduced. In the early stages of immigration, little additional social overhead capital was required to be provided to match the added labour force, as the migrants consisted mainly of young males who could be housed in dormitories, and who needed few amenities such as schools and hospitals. With the passage of time, and the replacement of single men by families, immigration produced an external public diseconomy to offset part or possibly all of the gain from lower wages and higher profits in the private sector.

In Germany, the cut-off of immigration had both social and economic bases. In the 1966 recession, the continued inflow of workers was interrupted because of rising unemployment. A second interruption took place in the 1975-76 recession, but this time German opinion seems to have resolved not to renew the inward movement when recovery took place, largely for social reasons. Towns with more than 12 percent of the labour force as foreign "guestworkers" were told they would be allowed no more. Families of existing immigrant workers were allowed to enter on humanitarian grounds, but anxiety was beginning to be felt about the difficulties of absorbing foreign workers into German society. Few of them learned German, and the children of many of them grew up, unassimilated, without German education or language. Rules against employing such children were relaxed in due course. The conflict nonetheless remains between the economic stimulus of guestworkers and their cultural lack of assimilation, particularly of Yugoslavs and Turks whose cultures were more dissimilar to the German than the Italian, Spanish, Portuguese, or that most assimilable people, the Greeks.

35

My attempt at applying the Lewis model to Italy was question-
ed by Giacomo Vaciago, who maintained that Italian rapid
growth in the 1950s and 1960s was the result of reallocating resources from slow-growing to fast-growing industries, not unlimited supplies of labour, and who observed that Italian growth
did not slow down in 1963 as I predicted it would.[1] On the first
score, the difference between us seems insubstantial. Edward
Denison, in his *Why Growth Rates Differ*, also ascribes a leading
role to resource reallocation,[2] but he has suggested to me pri-
vately that he and I are saying the same thing in different ways.
On my poor forecast, premature by five years, I acknowledge
error.

It should be noted that Italy also encountered social problems,
and not only when Italian workers crossed the Alps. The workers of the Mezzogiorno who transplanted themselves to the
"Golden Triangle" of Genoa-Turin-Milan, faced problems of
social assimilation too, as is well known. Recognizable because
of their smaller stature and darker complexion, they met social
discrimination at the same time that they were sought after
economically to hold down wages, maintain profits, stimulate
investment and growth. The suggestion has even been made that
Italians from the Mezzogiorno working outside Italy were less
alienated and distressed than those in the North. Both worked
hard, saved much, scrimped on consumption, sent funds back
to their families and relatives and met with discrimination.
Those outside Italy, however, had no expectation that they
would be assimilated, while those in Northern Italy were unhappy at being scorned in their own country.

Just as in the Lewis model, the transfer of labour from the agricultural to the industrial sector increases economic growth in
both areas, as profits and investment rise in industry and reduced
working forces raise income per capita in agriculture, so international migration in Europe after World War II helped economic growth in the countries of emigration as well as in those of

1. GIACOMO VACIAGO, 'Alternative Theories of Growth and the Italian Case',
Banca Nazionale del Lavoro Quarterly Review, vol. XXIII, No. 93, June 1970, pp. 180-211.

2. EDWARD F. DENISON, *Why Growth Rates Differ. Postwar Experience in Nine Western
Countries*, Washington, D.C.: Brookings Institution, 1967.

immigration. Until the flow of migrants was turned off, emigration added to income per capita, to growth and helped the balance of payments on current account in Southern Italy, Spain, Portugal, Greece, Turkey, and, I believe, Yugoslavia. The rate of saving on migrants' income was high, and much of it was remitted to the home country. It is understandable that Turkey and Jugoslavia both face difficulties of meeting debt service on foreign borrowings after the rapid decline in emigrant remittances.

The Greek case is worth particular attention. The Greeks have long been migrants, and have moved in a sort of diaspora to the corners of the earth, to North America and Australia, as well as throughout Europe. This migration reduced underemployment and unemployment in Greek cities, raised the marginal return on labour to the wage rate, encouraged new investment in Greece, and stimulated growth. In due course, the outflow of labour slowed down, a return flow was set in motion, and today it is said that Greece has shifted sides in the process and is importing labour on balance from poorer countries to undertake the dirty jobs in the country.

The iron law of wages, and its extension to the Lewis model of growth with unlimited supplies of labour, presupposes a single competitive market for labour. This is by no means an accurate description of reality, either historically or in the world today. An example is provided by the Irish worker in England, who had the worst jobs, the worst housing and the disdain, if not the hatred, of the English. In Switzerland, as I understand it, and as the Italian motion picture "Bread and Chocolate" so eloquently states, the immigrants belong to a non-competing group, assigned the dirty, menial, underpaid, and unattractive jobs of the economy. The proportion of these jobs in the economy will doubtless vary with the wage structure, culture, comparative advantage, level of income and a number of other variables. In a tourist country like Switzerland, waiters, bellboys and chambermaids comprise a significant proportion of the labour force with jobs that can be filled only with foreign workers. Other industries that rely heavily on immigrants are agricultural labour, construction, assembly-line manufacture, dirty assignments in dye factories and slaughterhouses, urban services such as street cleaning, refuse handling and the like. It was suggested that Switzerland was prepared to slow down its growth when native-born Swiss, except for peasant proprietors, have largely been pushed up the social ladder into the middle class. The abler and more effective of the migrants would have difficulty breaking out of the lower strata of the working class, because discrimination against them is stronger in white-collar occupations such as selling and office work.

If immigration is cut off for social reasons, how are the dirty jobs then handled? This is a question of no particular moment when Europe is in the economic doldrums; young people will accept disagreeable work temporarily as they wait for careers to open up. There are signs, however, that the problem is arising in Germany, with industry anxious to fill with foreigners slots that domestic workers are unwilling to accept. Partly the dirty jobs are not performed at all, or are undertaken by consumers. Housewives do their own cooking and cleaning on an increasing scale, as household service is harder and harder to find. Standards decline. In an affluent society, the streets become and stay dirty. Restaurants give way to cafeterias, and hotels with bellboys to motels in which guests carry their own luggage, as they must increasingly do at airports. In part the consumer is aided by labour-saving machinery, appliances in the home, wheels attached to luggage at the airport, mechanical sweepers to clean the streets, and tank-trucks to wash them. To some extent the wage scale for dirty jobs may become inverted as compared to the position in which the *Lumpenproletariat* is available to perform them. Coal-mining has gone from the lowest paid occupation in most countries before World War II to the highest paid afterwards. To a degree this was the result of trade union organization. To a greater extent, I believe, it reflected the fact that the non-competing group was no longer willing to stay apart, and had to be held in coalmining, or attracted to it, by much higher wages. This tendency may make appearance for the dirty industries as a whole and call for a changed wage structure. When and if that does happen – and one can see signs of it in Sweden – the pressure of the bulk of wage-earners, in unions or outside, to reconstitute the traditional wage structure with its traditional differentials, is likely to add a strong impetus to inflationary pressures.

The iron law of wages or the Lewis model rests on the empirically observed generalization that capital widening is an easier accomplishment than capital deepening. Growth is more readily produced by adding more labour at constant rates, or, more accurately, at wage rates that rise more slowly than productivity, than by substituting capital for labour. Of course the two paths to growth are difficult to disentangle. Widening of capital is inevitably capital deepening, as extension of capital at the margin uses the latest vintages of machinery. But the economists' *a priori* judgment that growth can be achieved either by capital widening or by capital deepening, or some intermediate combination of the two, seems to be belied by experience. Running out of labour interrupts the growth process, and causes the positive feedback process of virtuous circles to give place to setbacks as profits fall while wages rise. In a Schumpeterian world where falling profits stimulate innovation and investment, it might be easy to recover from running out of labour by a smooth transition to substituting capital for labour. In a Keynesian world where falling profits lead to cutbacks in output and recession, the result is far from assured.

Thus far we have been discussing cases where growth is stimulated exogenously in an industrial sector, or in a country as a whole, and is sustained there, and spread elsewhere, by transfers of workers from other sectors, whether agriculture or proto-industry at home, or a foreign country. The transfer need not be direct. In France, the labour that left shrinking agriculture went largely into services – both commercial and governmental – while the labour recruited by modern industry came largely from the *artisanat* – a highly inefficient non-competing portion of the industrial sector. These artisans were driven into industry by imports from the European Common Market, and by the outbreak of competition with modern industry that in its turn was forced to cut costs and lower prices to meet competition from custom-union partners.

5. The case when there is no exogenous source of growth

We can now consider the case of no exogenous source of growth – no technological change, capital inflows for investment, animal spirits on the part of entrepreneurs, even planning. It can happen that improving agriculture and population growth in the countryside produce an excess of workers in the rural community with no place to go. The Lewis model does not initiate growth. It sustains it once started. In these circumstances instead of growth with unlimited supplies of labour, we have unlimited supplies of labour without growth. This had been the human condition before, and for a long time during, the industrial revolution, with high numbers of vagrants, tramping artisans, beggars. It remains so today in many underdeveloped countries that build up pressure for emigration. Sometimes the pressure is relieved, as in the British West Indies and Mexico, where legal and illegal migration takes place to North America. If international migration is impossible, masses of people leaving agriculture crowd into bidonvilles, favellas, barrios, or Hoovervilles – as they were called in the United States at the depth of the depression – shantytowns erected on waste land around cities that pose difficult social and political problems of health, sanitation, crime and political turbulence. This is a very general problem that can be seen in the Speenhamland system of poor relief in Britain enacted in 1795 and replaced in 1834, and in the Fascist legislation limiting the movement of labour in Italy in the 1920s. Both were attacked as dictatorial and cruel, but both addressed the problem that keeping unemployed or underemployed labour on the farm, in the village or parish, at least meant that it would be provided with shelter, and if a farming family, with food (out of the rent of the farm). In the city, on the other hand, there were no jobs, no shelter and no food, unless the hard-pressed state provided it. Today city planners respond to the social tragedy implicit in this movement by arguing for the construction of model cities, with decent inexpensive housing. The objective is unexceptionable; the only question is whether scarce capital would not better applied to productive ends, rather than to consumption.

A similar agonizing choice arises today in economic development over whether plans should concentrate on increasing productivity and income of those employed, or allocating capital and effort so as to take the unemployed and underemployed into useful work in order to distribute income more equitably, and to raise minimum standards for the poorest segments of society in health, education, sanitation and housing. Some economists fail to see the conflict between faster growth on the one hand, and more equitable income distribution on the other, and demand both.[1] In a few cases growth and equity may be complements rather than substitutes. Such would be the case if the working classes had as high a marginal propensity to save as the entrepreneurial, whether because the poor save, as in Germany, or the rich spend their incomes on conspicuous consumption, as is true of a number of less-developed countries. It was once said that Mexico was the happiest of all countries with high profits that were reinvested, and revolutionary slogans to keep the working classes content. While Mexican growth is under way, neither aspect of that once happy state seems to obtain: the rich live opulent lives, and the poor grow restive.

It is worth thinking about the industrial revolution in Britain once more. Observing it from the Continent, Germans and French coveted the sharp increase in productivity, but, like Engels, deplored the vile conditions to which the working classes had to submit, and from which they revolted on many occasions from Peterloo in 1819 to the Chartist riots of the 1840s. It is salutary to recall that much of this unrest was the result of the breakdown of the guild system, based on handicrafts operating in monopolized markets, and of the suffering of proto-industry – independent cottage workers – under the competition of the factory. Enough of it, however, was the consequence of the iron law of

---

1. See, for example, the essay by OSVALDO SUNKEL, 'Latin American Under development in the Year 2000', in JAGDISH NATWARLAL BHAGWATI, ed., *Economics and World Order, from the 1970s to the 1990s*, New York: Macmillan, 1972, pp. 199-231: and GERALD HELLEINER's 'Introduction' to GERALD K. HELLEINER, ed., *A World Divided. The Less Developed Countries in the International Economy*, Cambridge: Cambridge University Press, 1976, pp. 1-28. For a contrary view, see CARLOS DIAZ-ALEJANDRO's 'The post 1971 international financial system and the less developed Countries', in JAGDISH NATWARLAL BHAGWATI, ed., *op. cit.*, which questions whether redistribution and growth are compatible (pp. 243-6).

wages, the Lewis or Marxian model of unlimited supplies of labour, or an industrial reserve army, which made growth continuous, except for periodic intervals of financial crisis. Over 100 years, it worked out well, and led to the highest level of living outside the empty spaces of America and the regions of recent settlement. But the ultimate achievements of growth can have been small consolation to the successive generations of working men and women that had to wait for their great grandchildren to benefit. The position was helped in the early stages by the absence of expectations of higher levels of consumption, and toward the end, by aspirations of higher levels of living for children. In today's world in which modern communication shows how well some members of society live, the prospect that a rising standard of living must be postponed for several generations can readily be seen to lead to social unrest.

The iron law of wages in its Ricardian, Malthusian form is thus a heavy burden in much of today's underdeveloped world. It evidently calls for the family limitation that is getting increasing attention in India, China, Indonesia, Mauritius, Haiti, and elsewhere, though more is needed. For Europe I would claim that the Lewis model of growth with unlimited supplies of labour has great explanatory value for economic history, at least as far back as the 18th century, and through the 19th and 20th. Moreover, if Europe has come to the end of its local labour supplies, and is unwilling for social reasons to accept large numbers of would-be migrants poised on her periphery, continued growth may be threatened, or the nature of growth must be altered – a task that does not look easy.

THIRD LECTURE
Gresham's Law

1. Introduction. – 2. Market instability for different monies. – 3. Market instability and bank-note convertibility. – 4. Market instability and two central-bank reserve currencies. – 5. Real and financial assets: a generalized market instability problem.

1. Introduction

Once again in this lecture I am going to give the name of a "law" to something that is miscalled. Gresham's law – that bad money drives good money out of circulation – is misnamed because the empirical uniformity was not discovered by Gresham at all. It was wrongly attributed to him in 1857 by Henry D. McLeod. Raymond de Roover tells us that the principle was already well known in 1550, having been stated by Nicolaus Copernicus in his essay on coinage of 1525.[1] Louis Wolowski traces the idea back to Nicholas Oresme, Bishop of Lisieux in France, who wrote *De Moneta* in 1360 or so, attacking monetary debasement and asserting that the king had no right to change the weight or fineness of coins, or the bimetallic ratio.[2] An obscure British writer, Humphrey Holt, complained in 1551 that debased coins were driving good heavy coins abroad and pushing up prices. This was the year in which Sir Thomas Gresham went to Antwerp as a private merchant and royal factor, or financial agent of the Crown, paying out the service of old debts, buying ordnance against new, and handling specie payments. As is so often the case, the rich, prominent man gets the credit for well-known theories devised by others.

It is of course too late to change the appellation of Gresham's law to the Oresme, the Copernican or the Holt law. I want, moreover, to widen the scope of Gresham's law first to two monies, and then beyond it to discuss market instability, whether for dif-

---

1. RAYMOND ADRIEN DE ROOVER, *Gresham on Foreign Exchange*, Cambridge, Mass.: Harvard University Press, 1949, pp. 91-2.

2. LUDWIG (LOUIS) FRANCISZEK MICHAL RAIMOND WOLOWSKI, *La Question monétaire*, Second edition, Paris: Guillaumin, 1869, p. 19.

ferent monies, as in bimetallism, for notes and coins, two central-bank reserve assets, and the like, to two different sorts of assets more generally, and especially to money on the one hand, and real or other types of financial assets on the other. Gresham's law thus extended is a highly useful analytical model for the economic historian to keep in his toolbox, although as the theme of these lectures warns, it is but one among many, rather than a universal solvent, or sovereign remedy, like holy relics or North American snake oil.

Gresham's law gained acceptance in a period when most money was silver and the problem lay in the difficulty of keeping good and bad coins together in circulation side by side. Coins that had been sweated, clipped, rubbed, worn or otherwise reduced in weight, or adulterated by addition of other metals and subtraction of silver would be spent quickly. Good coins would be hoarded or shipped abroad where they were sold for their specie weight rather than their nominal value.

Discussion of Gresham's law in this generation has mostly concerned the gold-exchange standard, under which central-bank reserves consisted of gold, foreign exchange convertible into gold, or both, and the trade-off runs between an appropriate supply of international money on the one hand, and its instability with two sorts of reserves on the other. Earlier, the issue arose mainly in connection with bimetallism, where again instability from having two monies – gold and silver – was judged acceptable or unacceptable depending upon one's judgment as to the significance of instability on the one hand and a larger money supply on the other. The trade-off between quantity and stability, however, fails to get to the root of the issue. There is the further vital point that the same money does not always serve with equal efficiency in all uses. More monies may be needed not only to get the quantity right, but to provide the appropriate monies for the different purposes for which they are most suitable.

In the Middle Ages, three metals were used as money – to ignore the sporadic and occasional use of salt, pepper, barter, book entries, tokens, truck, bank notes and bills of exchange – namely copper, silver and gold. Copper was required for small retail transactions of simple folk, but did not suit as well the larger expenditures of middle-class and noble households that used silver, nor the still larger transactions of great merchants that were most efficiently settled in bills of exchange, but where these were unavailable, in gold. Gold was useless for the peasant or craftsman; copper, as Swedish merchants and banks learned the hard way, was a most awkward money for use in settling international imbalances.[1] In France, copper was legal tender up to 1/40th of debts to assist those receiving it to pass it along, but the royal Treasury still found itself overwhelmed with more than it could use. The *Régie des Postes* under Napoleon I, for example, received 9 millions out of its 10 million livres of annual receipts in copper.[2] And of course Gresham's-law problems grew as one moved from metallic monies to bills of exchange, bank notes, deposits, certificates of deposits, and the like. All are money, or may be under appropriate definitions. Most have a comparative advantage in one or another use. The problem is to ensure that they are continuously convertible into one another at fixed rates, the fixed rates being the essence of being able to continue counting them as money.

1. ELI F. HECKSCHER, 'The Bank of Sweden in its Connection with the Bank of Amsterdam', in J. G. VAN DILLEN, ed., *History of the Principal Public Banks*, The Hague: Martinus Nijhoff, 1934, pp. 161-89, see pp. 179-80.
2. FRANÇOIS NICOLAS MOLLIEN, *Mémoires d'un Ministre du Trésor Public, 1780-1815*, Paris: Fournier, 1845, tome III, p. 171.

2. Market instability for different monies

If we move a slight distance from money, Gresham's law could be extended to cover many kinds of assets in portfolios, with the problem to ensure that money can be exchanged for the assets, or the assets for money, and if not at fixed prices, at least at prices that do not careen about wildly. This issue will be dealt with later; bimetallism will be examined first, then the convertibility of notes into coin and deposits into notes, and finally the gold-exchange standard and the pure exchange standard will be touched upon.

Gold has always had a certain magical quality to it, familiar from the Midas legend, and evoked by the heading in one of Keynes' chapters in *The Treatise on Money*, and again in *Essays in Persuasion*, "*auri sacra fames*", or the sacred mystique of gold.[1] Silver may not arouse such deeply psychoanalytical feelings. For the most part, in the last century or two, the contest has been between the gold standard as such, and bimetallism. A number of poorer countries, notably India, China, and Mexico, have embraced the silver standard in the past as Europe had done until 1700 or so; American experiments in raising the price of silver under the New Deal to appease the silver Senators proved deeply disturbing to China and Mexico which were then still on the silver standard.[2]

In 1819 a number of Britons urged that the country resume specie payments in silver, not gold. A number more seem to have preferred the bimetallic standard but fell back on gold as a second-best solution so as to avoid rendering comfort to the monetary cranks who urged against resumption and in favour of continued inconvertibility.[3] In the 1850s in California and Austra-

---

1. JOHN MAYNARD KEYNES, *A Treatise on Money*, London, Macmillan 1930, vol. II, Chapter 35; *Essays in Persuasion*, New York: London, Macmillan, 1932, p. 181; respectively reprinted in *The Collected Writings of John Maynard Keynes*, vol. VI, *A Treatise on Money: The Pure Theory of Money*, Chapter 35 and vol. IX *Essays in Persuasion*, p. 248, London: Macmillan, 1971 and 1972.

2. See CHARLES P. KINDLEBERGER, *The World in Depression, 1929-1939*, Berkeley: University of California Press; London: Allen Lane, The Penguin Press, 1973, p. 235.

3. The secondary sources are a little confused as to which economists or economic amateurs favoured silver and which bimetallism. Smart states that the Earl of Lau-

lia gold discoveries threatened to cheapen gold relative to silver and gave rise in France to three successive commissions investigating the monetary standard problem. One member of the commissions, Michel Chevalier, recommended demonetizing gold and moving to the silver standard, as opposed to one member, Esquirou de Parieu, recommending demonetizing silver and the remaining four members coming out for retention of bimetallism.[1] One metallic money as a rule meant gold, adopted by Britain *de facto* in 1774, and *de jure* 42 years later. Two monies meant bimetallism, with gold and silver coins circulating side by side at some fixed mint ratio. Problems arose from many sides; from the fact that mint ratios might differ between countries, although this was not serious so long as transport costs were fairly high and kept the export and import points of the two metals wide apart; from uneven debasement of coins in the separate metals; and especially from changes in production in gold and silver reflecting the accidental effects of discoveries and new mining processes. I say "accidental", although it should be recalled that the age of exploration, initiated by Henry the Navigator of Portugal and culminating in Columbus' discovery of America, was a response, conscious or subconscious, to the 15th-century shortage of specie, brought about by the need to export metal to the Levant in payment for import surpluses.[2]

The ratios at which gold and silver have been coined and thus

---

derdale favoured silver over gold (WILLIAM SMART, *Economic Annals of the Nineteenth Century*, vol. I, *1801-1820*, London: Macmillan, 1910-1917; reprinted New York: Augustus M. Kelley, 1964, pp. 478, 622). In one discussion, Fetter notes that the Earl of Lauderdale introduced a resolution for bimetallism (FRANK WHITSON FETTER, *Development of British Monetary Orthodoxy, 1797-1875*, Cambridge, Mass.: Harvard University Press, 1965, p. 9). In a more recent work he observes that Alexander Baring, Peter King, the Earl of Lauderdale, Poulett Thompson, and Sir Robert Richard Torrens, in principle supporters of a silver standard or of bimetallism, held back because of their strong opposition to inconvertible paper money (FRANK WHITSON FETTER, *The Economist in Parliament, 1780-1868*, Durham, N.C.: Duke University Press, 1980, p. 95).

1. LOUIS WOLOWSKI, *La Question monétaire, op. cit.*, pp. 187-8.

2. RALPH DAVIS, *The Rise of the Atlantic Economies*, Ithaca: Cornell University Press, 1973, pp. 4, 7. See also PIERRE VILAR, *A History of Gold and Money, 1450-1920*, translated from the 1969 French edition by JUDITH WHITE, London: NLB, 1976, pp. 45, 47, 63; first published as *Oro y Moneda en la Historia, 1450-1920*, Barcelona: Ediciones Ariel, 1969.

exchanged for one another have ranged widely. The easily available records beginning in the 13th century show the ratio falling from about 12 ½ silver to 1 of gold in 1244, to a little over 11 to 1 just before Columbus' discovery. With gold pouring in from Brazil in the first half of the sixteenth century, the ratio fell to 5 to 1. The subsequent flood of silver from the mines of Mexico and Peru tilted the ratio back to more than 15 to 1. In 1717, when Sir Isaac Newton was Master of the Mint in London, a price of gold was set that lasted 200 years. Dominant money at the time was silver. The gold standard began in Britain when silver was demonetized, except for coins, *de facto* in 1774, *de jure* in 1816.[1] Bimetallism was retained in France, with frequent fine adjustments in the 18th century under Turgot and Mirabeau, leading, after the monetary difficulties of the Revolution, to the establishment of the franc under the Law of 7 Germinal (1803). Paris became the European pivot for gold and silver. It came to the aid of London in the crisis of 1825, for example, exchanging gold largely in sovereigns for silver when the Bank of England was having difficulty in keeping its notes convertible into gold coin.[2] The gold discoveries in California and Australia proved less disturbing than Michel Chevalier thought would be the case because gold arriving from overseas in London was rapidly shipped to Paris which offset its impact on the quantity of money in Western Europe by losing silver to the Far East. In 1860 when silver was overvalued, the Bank of France exchanged £2 million of silver for gold with the Bank of England in order to have enough gold on hand to avoid paying out silver. For it to have paid out silver would have caused a run on bank notes exchanged for silver.[3] Again in 1876 the Bank of France was embar-

1. UNITED STATES SENATE, *International Monetary Conference*, held in Paris, in August 1878, under the auspices of the Ministry of Foreign Affairs of the Republic of France, Senate Executive Document No. 58, 45th Congress, Third Session, Washington D.C.: Government Printing Office, 1879, p. 619; reprinted New York: Arno Press, 1979.

2. Sir JOHN CLAPHAM, *The Bank of England: A History*, Cambridge: Cambridge University Press, 1945, vol. 2, p. 100.

3. WALTER BAGEHOT, 'The Effects of the Resumption of Specie Payments in France on the Price of Silver', in *The Silver Question*, IV, *The Economist*, vol. XXXIV, 18th March 1876; reprinted in *The Collected Works of Walter Bagehot*, edited by NORMAN ST JOHN-STEVAS, London: The Economist, 1978, vol. X, pp. 150-5, *see* p. 150.

rassed by having its principal reserve in the appreciated metal – this time gold – but resolved the issue not through acquiring and paying out silver, but by abandoning bimetallism for the gold standard.[1]

The discoveries in California and Australia yielded as much gold in ten years as had been produced in the 356 years between 1492 and 1848.[2] A somewhat different calculation by Knut Wicksell concludes that in the 25 years after 1851 the world produced as much gold as in the previous 250.[3] Whatever the calculation, the discoveries led to an intense discussion in France of the wisdom of bimetallism, as already indicated, and in particular a sharp debate between the bimetallist Louis Wolowski and the monometallist Michel Chevalier. Ludwig Bamberger, who was in France at the time, stated that men lose their wits about two things, love and bimetallism.[4] Forty years later the polemic between Karl Helfferich, monometallist, and Otto Arendt, the leading German supporter of the Junker bimetallist position, became so heated that Arendt sued Helfferich for slander (but had his suit thrown out of court).[5] In the debate with Chevalier, Wolowski used some striking metaphors. He quotes Molière's *Le Malade Imaginaire*: "Me, cut off an arm, pluck out an eye, in order to get along better. What a beautiful operation – make myself blind and crippled."[6] And he quotes another bimetallist, Cernuschi, who asked: "The world offers two fuels; is it necessary to proscribe wood because one burns coal?"[7]

These rhetorical questions may be said to pose the issue. If two

---

1. *Ibid.*, p. 152, and UNITED STATES SENATE, *op. cit.* 207n.

2. MICHEL CHEVALIER, *On the Probable Fall in the Value of Gold: The Commercial and Social Consequences which may Ensue, and the Measures which it Invites*, translated from the French, with Preface, by RICHARD CORBEN, Manchester: Alexander Ireland & Co., London: W. H. Smith and Son; Edinburg: Adam and Charles Black, Third edition, 1859, p. VI.

3. KNUT WICKSELL, *Lectures on Political Economy*, vol. II, *Money*, New York: Macmillan; London: G. Routledge & Sons, 1935, p. 37.

4. Quoted by PAUL H. EMDEN, *Money Powers of Europe in the Nineteenth and Twentieth Centuries*, New York: D. Appleton-Century, 1938, p. v.

5. JOHN G. WILLIAMSON, *Karl Helfferich, 1872-1924, Economist, Financier, Politician*, Princeton: Princeton University Press, 1971, pp. 33-5.

6. LOUIS WOLOWSKI, *La Question monétaire, op. cit.*, p. 91n.

7. *Ibid.*, p. 217.

monies are complements, and more is better than less, as agrarian interests like the Junkers in Germany and the Populists in the United States believed, then two monies are better than one. If, on the other hand, the two monies are substitutes, and expectations as to which is the more valuable tilt back and forth and lead to hoarding or exporting one, stepping up the spending of the other, one is better than two. Some monometallists, and hard money men who oppose the use of bank notes, or of foreign exchange as central-bank reserves along with specie, base their opposition to two monies on fear of inflation. Some bimetallists objected to the gold standard for fear of deflation, notably the eloquent William Jennings Bryan. The Gresham's-law question ignores the appropriate quantity of money, that is regarded as separable, and focuses on instability. Walter Bagehot held that bimetallism was not a currency of two metals, but a system of alternative currencies.[1] A defender of bimetallism like Wolowski calls it not a double standard, but double money.[2] Rhetorical tricks abounded. Alfred Marshall sought to overcome the instability and at the same time gain the advantage of a larger monetary base by proposing "symmetallism", in which gold and silver would be always combined in coins and bullion in the same proportions – though this suggestion probably underestimated the ease of melting down the alloy and separating the metals if the market price diverged from the implicit ratio of the combination.[3] A similar proposal in effect was put forward to stabilize the gold-exchange standard by the Dutch economist, S. Posthuma, who recommended a rule that central banks should hold, pay out and accept gold and foreign exchange in their international reserves in an agreed fixed proportion.[4] Both these ideas rely on John Hicks' theorem that two commodities always traded at the same price may be regarded as one. An early at-

1. WALTER BAGEHOT, 'Bimetallism', in *The Silver Question*, XVII, *The Economist*, vol. XXXIV, 30th December 1876; reprinted in *The Collected Works of Walter Bagehot*, *op. cit.*, pp. 215-17, see p. 216.

2. LOUIS WOLOWSKI, *La Question monétaire*, *op. cit.*, p. 207.

3. ALFRED MARSHALL, *Money, Credit and Commerce*, London: Macmillan, 1923, pp. 64-7.

4. SUARDUS POSTHUMA, 'The International Monetary System', *Banca Nazionale del Lavoro Quarterly Review*, No. 66, September 1963, pp. 239-61.

tempt to stabilize the overvalued metal is found in the order issued by Charles V of Spain in 1514 that all bills of exchange be paid two-thirds in gold to make up for a decline in the circulation of gold coin.[1]

Bimetallism broke down after 1875, whether because of the discovery of the Comstock lode in Nevada in 1859, the new electrolytic process of recovering silver from lower-grade ores, the large-scale export of silver from Italy preceding the *corso forzoso* of 1866, the precipitous German switch from bimetallism to the gold standard after receiving the 500 million mark metallic portion of the indemnity after the Franco-Prussian war largely in gold, and dumping silver on the world markets, or some combination of the above. Long before this, however, Gresham's law had been tested many times in the convertibility of bank notes into coin.

1. FRANK C. SPOONER, *The International Economy and Monetary Movements in France, 1493-1725*, Cambridge, Mass.: Harvard University Press, 1972, p. 133.

3. Market instability and bank-note convertibility

Maintenance of bank-note convertibility is not perhaps exactly the same issue as that posed by two types of metallic money, since paper money has a comparative advantage over coin in terms of convenience and ease in counting, guarding, transporting. It is well to remember that in the early days of banking, bank deposits generally went to a small premium over coin because of this advantage and because of the implicit guarantee by the bank that the metallic reserves against the deposits consisted of the appropriate weight and fineness.[1] Moreover, paper and specie are not additive as are gold and silver, if the paper money is issued against reserves of coin or bullion rather than circulating side by side with it. Nonetheless, the principle is the same and the instability question is central. Instability can also be found between bank deposits and notes, bank deposits and specie, deposits of one bank and those of others. It is seldom that one finds instability between different denominations of bank notes issued by the same authority and in virtually infinitely elastic supply, but Gresham's law generalized a limited distance – I go further later – holds that there may be instability between any two forms of money. Wolowski summarizes Gresham's law in the expression *"le papier chasse le numéraire"* (paper money drives out specie), but one can find opposite cases in addition to the premium of paper over coin under early deposit banking just mentioned. Forrest Hill of the University of Texas tells me that during the 1860s when the rest of the United States was on the greenback standard because of the Civil War, California remained on gold for local payments and maintained a market in greenbacks needed for some payments to the federal government. In this instance, the strong currency drove out the weak, or gold chased paper, and Professor Hill regards it as the opposite of the traditional formulation of Gresham's law.[2]

It is perhaps far-fetched to subsume the Banking School vs.

---

1. J. G. Van Dillen, 'The bank of Amsterdam', in J. G. Van Dillen, ed., *History of the Principal Public Banks, op. cit.*, pp. 91-2.
2. Conversation with Professor Forrest Hill, Austin, Texas, 2nd April 1979.

the Currency School debate of the first half of the 19th century in Britain under the heading of Gresham's law, or the comparable modern debate of monetarists vs. Keynesians, but something of a case could be made for so doing. Like the bimetallists, the Banking School, Keynesians and expansionists on the whole do not give much weight to instability, and are more interested in enlarging the money supply, increasing spending, expanding incomes and employment. The Currency School and some monetarists worry somewhat about inflation, but are also concerned with instability and maintaining convertibility.[1] Convertibility of one money into another, of money into assets, and of normally marketable assets into money is the touchstone. When such convertibility is maintained, Gresham's law is held at bay. Monetary debate in the 19th century spent endless hours and countless pages discussing the conditions under which convertibility could be maintained, and forced circulation of bank notes avoided, whether by a 100 per cent reserve at the margin above a fiduciary issue, as under the Bank Act of 1844 in Britain, or a fractional reserve system, such as the *de facto* ratio of bank notes no more than three times the specie reserves of the Bank of France. A few unreconstructed fundamentalists opposed bank notes altogether – Henri Cernuschi in France wanted to limit them to amounts of specie on deposit in a reversion to 100 per cent deposit banking of the 17th century.[2] The agrarian radical, William Cobbett, in England opposed banking altogether,[3] and President Jackson in the United States was at the same time a populist who wanted monetary expansion, and a gold bug who opposed both banks and bank notes.[4]

The Gresham's-law clash between coin and bank notes ended

---

1. See CHARLES P. KINDLEBERGER, 'Keynesianism vs. Monetarism in the eighteenth- and nineteenth- centuries', in *History of Political Economy*, vol. 12, No. 4, Winter 1980, pp. 499-523.

2. See the testimony of GARNIER-PAGES, Ministère des Finances et Ministère de l'Agriculture, du Commerce et des Travaux Publics, *Enquête sur les principes et les faits généraux qui régissent la circulation monétaire et fiduciaire*, Paris: Imprimerie Impériale, 1867, tome II, p. 43.

3. MICHEL CHEVALIER, *Lettres sur l'Amérique du Nord*, Third edition, Paris: Gosselin, 1838, vol. I, p. 73 note.

4. *Ibid.*, vol. I, p. 223.

inevitably in the demonetization of coin except for small transactions, and then with a substantial element of seignorage. Bank
notes (and deposits) became established as the real money.
Demonetization of gold, like that of silver, took time and proceeded in stages. Gold coin coexisted with bank notes in periods of
calm only among grandfathers at Christmas, and in the stockings
of French peasants, for whom, remembering John Law, the *as-
signats* and the inflations of two world wars, there was never any
calm. In moments of agitation, gold would be sought as a hedge
against the uncertain value of notes and bank deposits. There
was never enough on such occasions. When the deflationary
troubles came in the United States in 1933, the run on banks
made it necessary to call in gold at the old price, and forbid
further private possession. Coin and bullion were forbidden to
foreign-exchange arbitrageurs in March 1968, when the two-tier
system was established, with one price for gold among central
banks and another for private holders (outside the United States).
In August 1971, the United States refused to convert dollars into
gold. With the gradual auctioning off of the gold stocks of the
International Monetary Fund and the Federal Reserve System
demonetization became virtually complete. Gold was reduced
to a commodity – and a highly speculative one at that. With no
fixed price, it ceased to be money, and paper reigns supreme.

It should be observed once again that two monies are sym-
metrically unstable and not that specie always drives out paper.
The "Golden Avalanche" of 1936-37, occurred when the price of
gold had been raised from $20.67 to $35.00 and many participants in financial markets, including not a few central banks,
thought gold was priced too highly. Dollars were bought in the
not-so-rational expectation that the gold price would be lowered
again, and gold poured into the United States for months until
the steadiness of the United States Treasury and its refusal to
lower the gold price became evident.[1]

---

1. Frank D. Graham and Charles R. Whittlesey, *Golden Avalanche*, Princeton:
Princeton University Press, 1939; reprinted New York: Arno Press, 1979.

4. Market instability and two central-bank reserve currencies

En route to demonetization of gold, Gresham's law made itself felt in two aspects of international money, in the clash between gold and foreign exchange in central-bank reserves, and in the clash between two reserve currencies. The gold-exchange standard developed well before World War I (as Peter Lindert has demonstrated).[1] It was promoted by Montagu Norman of the Bank of England at the Genoa conference after that war.[2] After World War II it was submitted to strong attack by Robert Triffin and Jacques Rueff. Triffin called the system absurd and self-destroying on the ground that it encouraged the reserve centre to over-issue its money.[3] Rueff thought it inflationary and providing unfair advantage in seignorage to the reserve-centre country.[4] Neither emphasized the instability under Gresham's law which the existence of two international monies implies, although both proposed replacing the gold-exchange standard with a single money. Triffin wanted to establish a newly-created internationally-operated paper money, with gold demonetized and dollars funded into the new money through the International Monetary Fund, much the sort of process now contemplated in the so-called Substitution Account at the International Monetary Fund Rueff favoured a return to the pure gold standard, with gold revalued to provide a liquid replacement for the dollars expelled from the system, and countries committed thereafter to settle all balances in gold.

Neither Triffin nor Rueff recognized that in any system with one money that proves to be not completely satisfactory in all uses, the market will create additional money or moneys to suit its needs. In particular, if the national money of the leading

1. PETER H. LINDERT, 'Key Currencies and Gold, 1900-1913', Department of Economics, Princeton University, N. J.: *Princeton Studies in International Finance*, No. 24, August 1969.

2. Sir HENRY CLAY, *Lord Norman*, London: Macmillan, 1957; reprinted New York: Arno Press, 1979, p. 137.

3. ROBERT TRIFFIN, *Gold and the Dollar Crisis*, New Haven: Yale University Press, 1960.

4. JACQUES RUEFF and FRED HIRSCH, 'The Role and the Rule of Gold: An Argument', Department of Economics, Princeton University, *Essays in International Finance*, No. 47, June 1965.

country in international financial intercourse is excluded from official reserves in favour of an artificially-created reserve unit or repriced gold, it is virtually inevitable that the market will choose sooner or later to hold at least some reserves in foreign exchange which is spendable. The gold-exchange standard grew up because of the convenience of maintaining reserves in a form that can be used directly, without the necessity to convert them first. For the most part the market chooses to ignore the distinction Triffin and Rueff sought between a reserve currency and a vehicle currency. National money of the leading economic country has a comparative advantage over a pure reserve unit insofar as it can be spent directly. It is virtually impossible to limit international monies to one unless that money is accepted in monetary transactions in the major countries of the world. If officials decree only one international money, the market will produce more, and by so doing reintroduce Gresham's law. With two international reserve centres, the instability threat of Gresham's law is more pressing perhaps than with gold and one national dominant money. If we may abstract from gold and silver and postulate a world where sterling and dollars are used as international monies, there is inevitable latent instability. I do not mean to exaggerate. Sterling, dollar, franc, and other national money blocs may co-exist under reasonable conditions of stability, so long as each financial centre can discharge the necessary functions. But should the capacity of a currency like the pound to finance trade and provide capital look less certain for any reason – whether because of a climacteric in productivity, capital losses during a war, overvaluation of its exchange rate, or any other reason independent countries belonging to no bloc, and some countries whose ties to the bloc are weak, will turn to other financial centres to fulfil their needs. Paris and London competed for preeminence as the world financial centre during the 19th century, with London's dominance established finally, in the view of most observers, when France went off gold during the Franco-Prussian war.[1] New York's rivalry with London began

1. See WALTER BAGEHOT, *Lombard Street. A Description of the Money Market*, Chapter II, 'A General View of Lombard Street', London: H. S. King, 1873; reprinted in *The Collected Works of Walter Bagehot, op. cit.*, vol. IX, pp. 58-68, see pp. 63-4.

sometime before or during World War I in the judgment of most historians,[1] but I have found an expression of American braggadocio in challenging London as early as the crisis of 1857.[2] Today with the dollar weak, there is no immediately viable alternative in the Special Drawing Right or the European Currency Unit, but if and when one is produced by official negotiation, or a national currency such as the Deutschmark, the Swiss franc, the Japanese yen is preferred by the market and permitted to be held abroad, Gresham's-law instability will return. Some holders will convert; others will do it more subtly, spending the weak currency and collecting payments in the strong. The present position with the dollar weak and gold demonetized seems anomalous. My reading of history leads me to the conclusion that it will not persist long, and by long I mean five to ten years.

Foreign-exchange crises can be assimilated to Gresham's law, with the two monies representing one national money on the one hand, and all other currencies into which it is convertible on the other. As in other instances, the crisis comes from a change in expectations. It may be belated, or come slowly, or suddenly result from an untoward event, but what happens is that a currency thought strong is seen to be weak, or the contrary, and people rush out of or into the domestic money. In the classic German hyper-inflation, the currency initially depreciated slowly, as Germans and foreigners thought it would be restored to par, and then rapidly as their initial hopes and expectations were proved to be false.[3] The market may be composed of insiders and

---

1. See, for example, PAUL P. ABRAHAMS, *The Foreign Expansion of American Finance and its Relationship to the Foreign Economic Policies of the United States, 1907-1921*, New York: Arno Press, 1974, and KATHLEEN BURK, 'J. M. Keynes and the Exchange Rate Crisis of July 1917', in *Economic History Review*, vol. XXXII, No. 3, August 1979, pp. 405-16, see p. 409.

2. See "the late struggle of 1857 was in a great degree between New York and London, and has terminated to the advantage of the former city. And the time must ere long arrive, when New York, and not London, will become the financial center not only of the New World, but also to a great extent, of the Old World" from the NEW YORK HERALD, *The Revolution of 1857 – Its Causes and Results*, in DAVID MORIER EVANS, *The History of the Commercial Crisis, 1857-1858, and the Stock Exchange Panic of 1859*, London: Groombridge and Sons, 1859; reprinted New York: Augustus M. Kelley, 1969, p. 114.

3. See LEAGUE OF NATIONS, Economic, Financial and Transit Department, *The*

outsiders, each with different perceptions, the outsiders catching on only slowly to what the insiders are doing. The first to buy get low prices, and the first to sell get high, whereas the outsiders tend to buy high and sell cheap, thus losing money. Of course national monies need not be unstable simply because there are other monies into which they are convertible. I do not insist that Gresham's law always applies, so much as that it is always a possibility. History is replete with illustrations.

The issue arises especially in connection with flexible exchange rates. Many economists assert that there can be no such thing as destabilizing speculation, that markets are rational and daily set prices that take into account all possible available information, so that there is no overshooting of prices upward or downward, no sudden reversals of views, no price changes in absence of changes in the objective situation. The record of the exchange market since the adoption of floating in March 1973 would seem to belie that view, but to pursue the subject would lead me too far afield. I should like to state some of my beliefs on this issue: (i) with flexible exchange rates there is no international money, so that the costs and benefits of international money are escaped and lost respectively; (ii) clean floating (or allowing the flexible exchange rate system to produce any exchange rate it chooses without intervention by the authorities) is an unworkable rule. I could go further and say that all strict rules are unworkable, but that too would lead me astray. For the moment I should like to say that intervention by the authorities in the determination of the exchange rate under a floating exchange rate regime is as inescapable as a lender of last resort in periods of domestic financial crisis.

To summarize, I claim that Gresham's law, which holds that two monies are unstable over time since the weak one drives the stronger into hoarding, is a fact of life virtually impossible to overcome because of the impossibility of settling for long on one money. There are two reasons for this. One money cannot discharge effectively all the tasks that money is needed for. The

Course and Control of Inflation. A Review of Monetary Experience in Europe after World War I, A Report written by RAGNAR NURKSE, League of Nations, 1946, p. 47.

money that suits one task may not fit another. In addition, if authorities attempt to fix the money supply, or leave it to nature to fix it by adopting a specific metal as money, the market will from time to time create new monies because it wants more. Metallic money led to banks and bank notes. The Bank Act of 1844, that fixed the supply of bank notes, stimulated the use of bills of exchange and bank deposits as money. If one fixes a certain M_i as money, and the market becomes excited, it will create an additional money M_j. The authorities insist on money as exogenous and fixed; if so the market will find new ways to monetize debt and make money endogenous and elastic and these new monies give us more than one money, paving the way for Gresham's law, and latent instability.

5. Real and financial assets: a generalized market instability problem

I now leave the field of exclusively monetary questions and widen the discussion to include other financial assets, and even real assets such as commodities, buildings and land. My contention is that a phenomenon so much like Gresham's law as to be included under its general heading may apply (but not necessarily) when money, other financial assets and real assets are not complements in a portfolio but substitutes because of expectations that their relative prices will change. As in the discussion of Gresham's law limited to money, we are dealing with crisis phenomena. Crises are not endemic; economies are not always unstable. I assert rather that crises may occur, and that history shows they have occurred. An economic theory that had no room for the instability implicit in Gresham's law would be incomplete, as would a view of economic history that assumed all markets were always in stable equilibrium.

Monetary economists assume that the demand for money is stable. They apply this in balance-of-payments analysis by suggesting that when the supply falls short of demand, people sell goods or securities abroad to build up their money stocks, and when supply at home exceeds demand, they spend the excess money on foreign goods or buy foreign securities to bring the supply of money down to the demand. This is of course a long-run view. In the short run, it makes little sense to vary output and spending to stabilize the supply of money when the evident function of money as a store of value is to bridge over discrepancies between income and spending. Moreover, the long-run view of monetarism that the demand for money is stable is sometimes falsified when people's expectations of the relative worth of money and other assets change, and households and businesses rush out of money into real and other financial assets, or out of real and other financial assets into money – in a sort of Gresham's law pattern of behaviour that leads them to dump one sort of asset for another.

In this sense the model is an ancient one. Adam Smith and John Stuart Mill called it overtrading, leading to revulsion and discredit.[1] Overtrading can take place in bonds, both foreign and domestic, stocks, real estate, both urban and rural, commodities, foreign-exchange (as already noted), particular forms of investment such as canals, railways, office buildings, shopping centres, holiday houses and the like. Lord Overstone is quoted by Walter Bagehot as having a somewhat longer sequence: "quiescence, next improvement, growing confidence, prosperity, excitement, overtrading, CONVULSION [Bagehot's capitals], pressure, stagnation, distress, ending again in quiescence",[2] that amounts to much the same thing.[3] Crises have been fewer in Britain after 1866, and in 1873 the British may have avoided one by fine tuning when the Bank of England discount rate was changed 24 times in a single year. But other countries and even Britain have had a number – 1873 in Austria, Germany and the United States, 1882 and 1888 in France, 1890 in Britain, 1893 in the United States, 1907 in Italy and the United States, 1920 in Britain, and again the United States in 1929, 1937 . . . There have been frequent foreign-exchange crises since World War II, and small bubbles in lending for 747 mothballed airplanes, oil tankers moored in Norwegian fjords or Greek bays, Real Estate Investment Trusts (REITS) and more recently mortgages, consumer credit, loans to less developed countries, and the gold bubble of last autumn 1979 and this winter 1979-1980, that reminded many commentators of the tulip mania of 1636, a third of a millennium earlier, and the silver bubble of spring 1980. Some event occurs, expectations are formed, they go too far, the market overshoots,

1. See ADAM SMITH, *An Inquiry into the Nature and Causes of the Wealth of Nations*, two volumes, London: Printed for W. Strahan and T. Cadell, 1766. The Edition quoted is the text edited by EDWIN CANNAN and published by Methuen & Co, London: Fourth edition, 1935 p. 406; JOHN STUART MILL, *Principles of Political Economy, with some of their applications to social philosophy*, First edition in two volumes, London: John W. Parker, 1848; The edition quoted is the text edited by W. J. ASHLEY, London: Longmans Green & Co., 1909, pp. 631-734.

2. WALTER BAGEHOT, 'Investments', *Inquirer*, vol. XI, No. 526, July 31 1852, p. 482; reprinted in *The Collected Works of Walter Bagehot, op. cit.*, vol. IX, pp. 272-5; see pp. 272-3.

3. O'Brien calls this one of the first statements of the trade cycle. It is contained in Lord OVERSTONE (then SAMUEL JONES LOYD), *Reflections Suggested by a Perusal of Mr. J. Horsley Palmer's pamphlet on the Causes and Consequences of the Pressure on the Money Market*. London: Pelham Richardson, 1837. See DENIS PATRICK O'BRIEN, 'Introduction' in DENIS PATRICK O'BRIEN, ed., *The Correspondence of Lord Overstone*, Cambridge: Cambridge University Press, 1971, vol. I, p. 63.

and then gradually, or suddenly, expectations are revised by a few or by the many, and the rush into some less liquid financial asset (than money) comes to a halt and the rush out of it into money begins. It may be thought that the difference between these financial crises and Gresham's law is considerable and, if pressed, I should have to concede that it may be so. With two monies, the official price is wrong, so that the market rushes to take advantage of it by spending the undervalued and hoarding the overvalued. With financial or commodity crises, there is no official price to be wrong. But there is something not too wide of that, that is, a sudden change in expectations which makes the old price in the market wrong, and a rush to get out of the overvalued security, asset or commodity into the safer one, money, before the price of the overvalued asset collapses.

Economic history teaches us that when Gresham's law relates to monies the possible remedies are several: 1) shift the mint price of the two metals nearer to the market price; 2) demonetize all but one of the monies; 3) increase the supply of the scarce money to show that you have enough to meet all contingencies; 4) increase the supply of the overvalued currency to ensure that you can meet all likely demands on the central bank with that and need not pay out the undervalued currency that guarantees profits to those who obtain it. Demonetizing all but one money, as already noted, has the awkwardness that it is unlikely that a single money – gold, silver, paper, foreign exchange – will meet all the money needs of the society. Increasing the supply of the scarce currency can be done from time to time by borrowing or swaps, but there are limits. Suspending local limits on paying out the abundant currency was the standard means of handling banking panics in Britain in the 19th century. The technique was to suspend the Bank Act of 1844 which required the Bank of England to maintain a fixed amount of gold against its bank-note liabilities. More generally in panics where there is a rush out of real and long-term financial assets into money, the means of allaying the panic is for the lender of last resort to make money freely available. Reassurance that other assets can be converted into money induces many asset holders to cease trying to convert them into cash. It is the prospect of a limit that excites panic selling, the fear that there will be no money left when it comes one's time to sell.

There is the view that markets always work well, and that there is no need for a lender of last resort. The historical response to this claim is to point to the facts of financial crises in history, and to emphasize that at the time, while the crises might in theory cure themselves if left alone, the authorities are rarely willing to take the risk that a given crisis will not. By some sort of revealed historical preference, the lender of last resort moves in panic, to provide the liquidity so desperately needed as judged by contemporaneous observers. William Huskisson said of December 1825, "We were within a few hours of a state of barter".[1] Clapham writing on the same panic said "It was as the Duke said of Waterloo, 'a damned nice thing' – the nearest run thing you ever saw in your life".[2]

It may well be that contemporaneous observers exaggerate the disasters that would ensue from failing to halt the panic. In 1933, the Bank Holiday in the United States was widely noted to have produced not dismay on the part of the public, but a relaxation of the inchoate financial fears of the previous months, and even a sort of carnival spirit that came from the release of tension. But I would argue that the possibility of sudden changes in expectations and normal relationships between the values of assets – in a sort of extension and generalization of Gresham's law – calls for an awareness of the role of the lender of last resort, at national and international levels, and that to dismiss such possibilities is irresponsibly to ignore the lessons of history.

Finally I should like to return to the narrower view of Gresham's law, and by way of conclusion re-emphasize the dilemma in which it puts us. With two or more monies, we are subject to the instability of Gresham's law. Any attempt to limit ourselves to one money is likely to be thwarted by the market's need for different monies for different purpose and its capacity to create them.

1. WILLIAM SMART, *Economic Annals of the Nineteenth Century*, vol. II, *1821-1830*, London: Macmillan, 1910-1917; New York: Kelley Reprints, 1964, p. 299.
2. Sir JOHN CLAPHAM, *The Bank of England: A History*, vol. II, *1797-1914*, Cambridge: Cambridge University Press, 1945, p. 101.

The market's capacity to create new monies raises an issue of monetary theory which has long been dormant but is nonetheless important to bear in mind. At the turn of this century, an issue of monetary theory centred on whether money was the creation of the state which typically had a monopoly of minting, often of issuing bank notes through its central bank, and regulated banks and through them deposits, or whether money was what money did, i.e. was a creation of the market. Knapp held to a state theory of money. The usage school held oppositely that while the state proposed, the market disposed. Money was what people used in making payments. On this showing, if the state issued a ukase that gold alone was money, the market could frustrate that decision by making payments with bank notes, bank deposits, bills of exchange, or other instruments. If the state then seeks to escape the clutches of Gresham's law by establishing a single money, this will work for money, provided that Knapp was right, and money is what the state determines it to be, but not for the instability of sudden panicky switches back and forth between money and other assets. If the usage school is right, however, as seems likely to me, the state can decree that there be one money, but the market can make more, thereby raising the possibility of Gresham-law instability, as switches occur between or among the various monies.

Under fixed exchange rates, despite Jacques Rueff's belief in gold settlements, the inconvenience of gold or Special Drawing Rights, or even the European Currency Unit, is virtually certain to make some national money superior for settling international payments, thus resulting in at least two monies, gold and a dominant national money. Since economies that wax may also wane, as the Gompertz curve derived from Engel's law in the first lecture makes clear, the dominant money that serves well for international payments at one time, may not suit so well in another era, thus inducing the market to switch over time to another currency. With two reserve currencies, Gresham's law is on the loose in another area. Reference can be made to the increasing unsuitability of the dollar as international money, and the attempt in the European Monetary System to create a viable alternative. The transition period between the world on the dollar standard and a shift to the ECU will be fraught with Gresham-law instability.

Perhaps Gresham's law and the possibility of instability have been overemphasized, for I maintain that for the most part markets are stable, and monies are stable. I only warn that Gresham's law explains a great deal of economic history. And it seems to me foolhardy to think of monetary reform as if Gresham's law could be wished away.

In his pamphlet on "A Universal Money" based on a series of articles in *The Economist* in 1868, Walter Bagehot started out proposing one universal money, and then backed off, thinking that it would take too much political will to integrate the pound, dollar, German mark on the one side and the Latin Monetary Union on the other:

> I fear the attempt to found a universal money is not possible now; I think it would fail because of its size. But I believe we could get as far as two moneys, two leading commercial currencies, which nations could one by one join as they chose, and which, in after time, might be combined; and though this may fall short of theoretical perfection, to the practical English mind it may seem the more probable for that very reason.[1]

I like the hint of the optimum currency area in the mention of size, and of John Williams' "key-currency" concept in the mention of "leading commercial currencies". But I would suggest to Walter Bagehot, and to the European Economic Community as its members set up the European Currency Unit, that economic history warns against the dangers of ignoring Sir Thomas Gresham's law, even if Gresham did not originally propound it.

1. WALTER BAGEHOT, *A Universal Money*, (*A Practical Plan for assimilating the English and American money, as a step towards a Universal Money*), London: Longmans, 1869; reprinted in *The Collected Works of Walter Bagehot, op. cit.*, vol. XI, pp. 57-104, see 'Preface', p. 66.

FOURTH LECTURE
The Law of One Price

1. Introduction. – 2. Markets and transport. – 3. Economic integration and factor-price equalization. – 4. Economic integration and money and capital markets. – 5. Economic integration and the elimination of intermediary marketing steps. – 6. The role of arbitrage. – 7. The problem of foreign direct investment. – 8. The optimum economic area. – 9. Conclusions.

1. Introduction

If I had named these lectures after individual economists – Engel, Arthur Lewis or Marx, and Gresham for the first three – this lecture would be entitled Smith's law, after Adam Smith. The law of one price states that in one market there is one price, from which it almost follows, but not quite, that when there is one price there is one market. Adam Smith put it that the division of labour was determined by the extent of the market.[1] Like him I am suggesting that a most powerful tool for observing the course of economic history is to examine the changing – for the most part growing – size of the market for goods, services, money and factors of production, including capital, labour, business enterprise, and if one is allowed to go beyond classical limits, ideas or information. The size of the market, moreover, is determined at any one time by the costs of overcoming distance and ignorance, by differences in tastes in private and public goods, and by the imposition or removal of natural or governmental barriers to the transport of outputs and inputs and to the dissemination of knowledge.

Our tradition in economics has been to concentrate unduly on trade policy, and on the imposition and removal of tariffs, subsidies, prohibitions and the like. Early definitions of economic integration identified it with free trade. But if integration means

---

1. ADAM SMITH, *An Inquiry into the Nature and Causes of the Wealth of Nations*, two volumes, London: Printed for W. Strahan and T. Cadell, 1766. The edition quoted is the text edited by EDWIN CANNAN, and published by Methuen and Co., London: Fourth edition, 1935, Book I, Chapter III, 'That the Division of Labour is Limited by the Extent of the Market'.

incorporation in one market, with one price, it is evident that markets may be separated in more ways than merely by government policy. Governments may discriminate by sources of supply and thus separate markets, but Nature and man may also discriminate, Nature by separating potential producers and consumers geographically, individual man by having different tastes for goods, occupations, habitats and the like, social man different tastes in public goods.

2. Markets and transport

One of the most powerful approaches to economic history is to observe changes in transport through time, and to see what this has done to the size and nature of markets.[1] Routes, modes, speed and costs of transport have continuously changed, for the most part to shorten routes, add new modes, increase capacity of existing carriers, shorten time and reduce costs, and to extend the market and make possible a greater division of labour. Like war and generals, the subject is too important to be left to location theorists. Adam Smith distinguished between ordinary trade and distant sale, the former on the whole being narrowly circumscribed in space, except for goods of high value for which it was worthwhile to overcome the costs of transport, the latter using cheap transport by sea.[2] At a time when coal doubled in price every 10 miles overland from the mines, it was used in Britain only where it emerged from the ground or at ports accessible to "sea coal". Cities like Bordeaux were intimately linked by sea with Saint Domingue in the West Indies, Nantes, Saint Malo, Le Havre and Marseilles in France, Amsterdam in the Netherlands, but were barely in touch for trade with places 50 kilometres in the interior. Edward Whiting Fox has suggested that for many purposes, political as well as economic, there were two Frances, one joined to the Atlantic trade, and juridically to Paris, the other consisting of a series of villages and towns, 40 kilometres or a day's horseback ride from one another, that shared the life of Atlantic France to a very limited degree.[3] In *Afterthoughts on Material Life* Fernand Braudel observes that there were three economies in early capitalism, one superimposed on the other: the subsistence economy rested at the base, with households engaged in performing most economic tasks at home, and dealing little in markets. On top of this was the capitalist economy, specializing and exchanging goods and services in largely local

1. WALTER ISARD, 'The General Theory of Location and Space Economy', *Quarterly Journal of Economics*, vol. LXIII, No. 4, November 1949, pp. 476-506.
2. ADAM SMITH, *The Wealth of Nations, op. cit.*, pp. 359, 381, 382, 393, etc.
3. EDWARD WHITING FOX, *History in Geographic Perspective. The other France*, New York: W. W. Norton & Co., 1971.

markets. The apex of the system was the world economy of distant trade.[1] The system endured longer than we are inclined to think. Eugen Weber believes that in France at least, the peasant became caught up in the national economy only between 1860 and 1880.[2] Prior to that time he was a purely local being, speaking patois not French, keeping accounts in *écus*, *sols*, *livres* and *liards* rather than in francs and sous, measuring with fathom, foot, ell, bushel, quart, pound and ounce, rather than the official metric system, and travelling so little that those who had been once to Paris were known as "Parisiens" for the rest of their lives. In the second half of the 19th century, this began to change, and peasants were gradually transformed into Frenchmen by roads, the railroad, military conscription in the war of 1870, and the spread of education.

Changes in transport produced discontinuous and dramatic changes in the size of the market. New routes – to the East via the Cape of Good Hope, the Suez Canal, and the Panama Canal – improvements in old forms of transport such as the Venetian rudder which made possible bigger sailing ships, the cog of the Hanseatic league, the fluit of the Dutch, not to mention the chronometer, steam engine, screw propeller, refrigeration, tankship, and ore carrier, and new forms of land transport like the stagecoach, canal, railroad, automobile, truck, airplane, led to new extensions of markets. As late as World War II, such products as steel had been strongly supply-oriented, traded for the most part within continents; after the war, they became footloose as a consequence of the giant ore carrier and the decline of general freight costs relative to steel, to such an extent that Japan can import iron ore from Australia and coal from the United States, and export the resulting steel up the Mississippi and Ohio rivers almost under the nose of Pittsburgh, that had been the locus for the original basing-point system for steel prices known as "Pittsburgh plus".

1. FERNAND BRAUDEL, *Afterthoughts on Material Civilization and Capitalism*, Translated by PATRICIA M. RANUM, Baltimore: Johns Hopkins University Press, 1977, Chapter 2.

2. EUGEN WEBER, *Peasants into Frenchmen. The Modernization of Rural France, 1870-1914*, Stanford, Cal.: Stanford University Press, 1976, *passim*, but especially Chapters 3, 6, 12, 17.

One aspect of change in transport unifying markets has been the increase in speed. Space can be measured in terms of days of travel. On this metric, the world has been continuously shrinking. Economic history has lately devoted enormous attention to the social saving in the innovation of the railroad. This is measured largely by adding up resources that would have been required to move the same goods by an alternative route, without attention to speed, flexibility and the like. In theory, increased speed can be regarded as a change in productivity, moving the isoquants of the production function in toward the origin, or as a change in the quantity or even the nature of output. It may also be labour or capital-augmenting. Social historians have not allowed increasing preoccupation with time since the Middle Ages to go unnoticed,[1] but changes in speed fit into economic analysis uneasily. Whatever the answers to the broader questions, there can be no doubt that faster movement of people and goods extends the market. In the 17th century, the Dutch built a series of canals for moving people at a pace which was fast then, slow by later turnpike standards, but above all dependable, enabling merchants to get from town to town on schedule, without the need to wait on wind and weather – a change in the nature of the output, and an extension of the market.[2] Michel Chevalier, who visited the United States in the 1830s to study public works, was vastly impressed by American emphasis on speed: "Commerce, for which time is money, was not content with merely quadrupling the speed of French navigable lines." Speed made it possible on western rivers to make three or four round trips a year instead of one. "That is important in a country which lacks manpower." Steam power on rivers and canals was a labour-augmenting innovation and one that strengthened ties between markets.[3] Before canals, steamships, railroads and the airplane, turnpikes reduced the time of journeys in Britain between the 1750s and 1830s by

1. See, for example, EDWARD PALMER THOMPSON, 'Time, Work-Discipline, and Industrial Capitalism', *Past and Present, a journal of historical studies*, No. 38, December 1967, pp. 56-97.

2. JAN DE VRIES, *Barges and Capitalism, Passenger Transportation in the Dutch Economy, 1632-1839*, Wageningen: A. A. G. Bijdragen, 1978.

3. MICHEL CHEVALIER, *Lettres sur l'Amérique du Nord*, Paris: Gosselin, Third edition, 1838, vol. II, pp. 15, 41.

80 per cent, constituting a transport revolution, and one that widened the market.[1]

For the most part, changes in transport costs are taken by economic historians to be exogeneous, or outside forces, but this is not necessarily so. Under a theory of linkages such as that developed by Albert Hirschman, innovations in transport leapfrog with those elsewhere in the economy.[2] The lateen (fore-and-aft) sail made it possible to tack more effectively in the trade winds, and for Henry the Navigator to get safely past Cape Bojador, the western-most land of Africa, and to discover the route to India around the Cape of Good Hope.[3] Hanseatic and Dutch trade requirements led to innovations in shipping and especially in shipbuilding.[4] The wider market for coal helped stimulate the steam engine to pump mine-water. In turn the steam engine, leading to the railroad and the steamship, widened the market for coal. A more cynical theory developed by Louis Girard suggests that each new method of transport destroys the rents of its predecessor, but in time raises prices so high in its own rent-seeking that it undermines its long-run welfare by encouraging competitive new entry. High charges of the turnpikes stimulated the canals, those of the canals in turn the railroad, and in due course, those of the railroad, the automobile and the truck.[5]

If we leave aside theories of innovation in transport, apart from the Isard view that they are pervasive in their impact on

1. PHILIP S. BAGWELL, *The Transport Revolution from 1770*, New York: Barnes & Noble, 1974, p. 42.

2. ALBERT O. HIRSCHMAN, *The Strategy of Economic Development*, New Haven: Yale University Press, 1958.

3. RALPH DAVIS, *The Rise of the Atlantic Economies*, Ithaca: Cornell University Press, 1973, pp. 5-6.

4. PHILIPPE DOLLINGER, *The German Hansa*, translated from the German and edited by D. S. Ault and S. H. Steinberg, Stanford: Stanford University Press (original 1964), 1970, Chapter 7; VIOLET BARBOUR, 'Dutch and English Merchant Shipping in the Seventeenth Century', *Economic History Review*, vol. II, No. 1, January 1930, pp. 261-90 (reprinted in WARREN C. SCOVILLE and J. CLAYBORN LA FORCE, eds., *The Economic Development of Western Europe*, Lexington, Mass.: Heath, 1970, vol. II, pp. 108-37).

5. LOUIS GIRARD, 'Transport', in HROTHGAR JOHN HABAKKUK and MOISEI MIKHAIL POSTAN, eds., *The Cambridge Economic History of Europe*, vol. VI, *The Industrial Revolutions and After: Incomes, Population and Technological Change*, Cambridge: Cambridge University Press, 1965, pp. 212-73.

the size of the market, what stands out is that more and more the individual producer firm and the individual consumer household are trading on the world market. Engel's law that growth lowers the income elasticity of demand for goods to less than one, and the need to consume services for the most part on the spot where they are produced, set limits to the overall proportions of consumption that may be drawn from the world economy at a distance, although tourism can take the consumer to the producer for many services. To a great degree, and especially in small countries, comparative advantage – the division of labour – is today conducted on a world scale, with the whole world serving as one market for goods with one price.

3. Economic integration and factor-price equalization

Thoroughgoing economic integration remains elusive, however. By economic integration I mean factor-price equalization achieved by direct trading on one market. Tinbergen's initial definition of integration was free trade.[1] This was unsatisfactory because, as already indicated, even where governments do not discriminate between suppliers or consumers, Nature and people may. Australia and Scandinavia are divided by distance, so that despite free trade between them, the range of tradeable goods would be limited, and the two markets for goods would not be effectively joined. Assume that governments encourage free intercourse and that countries are juxtaposed close to one another; people with differing tastes may still discriminate. Factor-price equalization is achieved through goods trade alone under certain limited circumstances which every graduate student is forced to memorize. Transport costs must be minimal, trade free, differences in tastes less pronounced than differences in factor endowments, markets competitive, goods more numerous than factors, each good unambiguously intensive of a particular factor, and so on. When these rigorous conditions are met, one price for each good in the two markets means one price for each factor in the two markets. Integration in the sense of factor-price equalization can then result either from factor movements, from goods movements, or from some combination of the two.

One more proviso should be added to the definition of economic integration as factor-price equalization. Where goods prices and factor prices in two countries are equated by trade or factor movements with a third country, without direct intercourse between the first and second countries themselves, one can hardly call price equalization so achieved "integration". Things equal to the same thing are equal to each other, but this equality has a fortuitous rather than a functional quality to it. To a considerable extent in recent years, prices for labour, capital and business enterprise in Europe have converged towards equality,

---

1. Jan Tinbergen, *International Economic Integration* (Second, revised edition), Amsterdam: Elsevier Publishing Company, 1965.

through each lining up with outside factors. Mediterranean labour moving between Germany and France has helped to bring German and French wages closer together, just as movement of capital between France and the Euro-currency market and between Germany and the Euro-currency market have aligned French and German interest rates to a degree without direct movement of capital between France and Germany. The term "integration" may still be appropriate to the wider entity – France, Germany and Mediterranean labour, or France, Germany and the Euro-currency market – but it is difficult to make much out of narrower Franco-German integration when factor-price integration takes place through goods trade with third countries, or factor movements with a third country, and little in the way of direct contact between principals.

It has long been clear that there has been little or no factor-price equalization between the industrialized world, as represented, for instance, by the membership of the Organization for Economic Cooperation and Development (OECD), and the Third World of developing countries. There is, in fact, a body of thought that regards such trade and investment as takes place between these groups as tending towards disintegration, driving centre and periphery in different directions and widening the income gap at least in absolute, if not in relative, terms. Gunnar Myrdal pointed out some years ago in *An International Economy* that social integration and not too wide a gap in factor incomes may lead to competitive trade, rather than competitive trade lead to factor-price equalization.[1] High-income countries are fearful of trading with low-income ones in products like textiles, shoes and increasingly electronics, steel and the like where advanced technology has been widely diffused. As in the abortive provision of the Kennedy round of the GATT that was prepared to reduce tariffs to zero in those products where the Common Market, the United States and Japan enjoyed 80 per cent of world trade, but not in others where developing countries had a significant stake, competition is welcomed only where it is not so intense, and a narrow

1. GUNNAR MYRDAL, *An International Economy: Problems and Prospects*, New York: Harper; London: Macmillan, 1956.

gap in incomes leads to competitive trade rather than *vice versa*.

For trade to take place on the scale necessary to approach world economic integration, there must be what Adam Smith called "magistracy", a minimum of law and order to forestall piracy, theft and violence, to enforce the discharging of obligations voluntarily entered into, rules not only for governments to follow in limiting their interference in trade, as under the GATT, but also in such questions as the law of negotiable instruments, clear understanding on weights and measures, agreements on acceptable standards, and most important, some form of international money, as a unit of account, medium of exchange, and store of value. Private trade, that is, takes place within a framework of public goods, of which an important element is the existence of money. One price that bespeaks a unified market requires some common mode of reckoning. The law of one price in goods thus leads out into monetary history and the history of international money and capital markets.

4. Economic integration and money and capital markets

As in goods, so in money, markets start small and grow in extent. McKinnon and Shaw, writing separately on the importance of wide, deep and efficient money and capital markets in developing countries, have renewed the interest of economic historians in the agglomeration of local and regional into national money and capital markets within countries, as well as international money, banking, lending and investment.[1]

The question was much on the minds of the citizenry of France in the 18th and 19th centuries, with many merchants and intellectuals seeking to spread banking outside the ports, Paris, and Lyons to the provincial cities and towns, and calling for regional banks of issue to supplement centralized institutions. Both in Britain and France, the central bank was attacked for working on behalf of the financial centre instead of the country as a whole. It was not unusual to have the Bank of England referred to as the Bank of London, the Bank of France as the Bank of Paris. John Law, Napoleon I, Jacques Laffitte, the Pereire brothers – indeed the entire school of Saint-Simoniens – shared what is referred to in the United States as the populist view, according to which Wall Street, the City of London, or the Paris financial community both exploits the rest of the country and ignores their interests.[2] Sir Thomas Roe, writing in 1640, said with reference to London and the rest of England: "It is no good for a body state to have a fat head, thin guts and lean members".[3] Economic development requires and brings about the spread of banking institutions more evenly through a country, more nearly equalizing rates of interest – which had been low in such places as Lyons and Paris, high in

1. RONALD I. McKINNON, *Money and Capital in Economic Development*, Washington, D.C.: Brookings Institution, 1973; EDWARD S. SHAW, *Financial Deepening in Economic Development*, New York: Oxford University Press, 1973.

2. CHARLES P. KINDLEBERGER, 'Keynesianism vs. Monetarism in Eighteenth and Nineteenth Century France', *History of Political Economy*, vol. 12, No. 4, Winter 1980, pp. 499-523.

3. Quoted by BARRY E. SUPPLE, *Commercial Crisis and Change in England, 1600-1642. A Study in the Instability of a Mercantile Economy*, Cambridge: Cambridge University Press, 1959, pp. 3-4.

intermediate centres such as Dijon or Lille. Domestic trade flourished where provincial borrowers had access to capital at more nearly uniform rates, and could collect their drafts anywhere, and not only in the financial capital.

5. Economic integration and the elimination of intermediary marketing steps

An important distinction must be made between structures in trade and those in money, as both in its own way follows the law of one price. Trade initially took place in stapling centres, such as Bruges, Antwerp, Amsterdam, London and the like, to which sellers came to dispose of goods, and buyers came to acquire them. The staplers were divided among the First Hand, who carried the goods to and from, say, Amsterdam in distant trade; the Second Hand, who broke bulk, graded, sorted, standardized, repacked, and sometimes in between arranged for finishing processes such as curing and roasting, and in textiles, fulling, sizing, washing, bleaching, dyeing and the like; and the Third Hand who distributed locally that small portion of imports that was not relayed further to other markets. Stapling was based on a monopoly of information, as to what goods were available, and what wanted, in both cases where, along with the secrets of finishing. With time, these monopolies were eroded as the information became diffused. Since transport costs were positive, and in some instances sizeable, once the monopoly of information was lost suppliers and consumers got together in direct trade with no further need to rely on the intermediation of the stapler. The finishing process could be conducted at either end, but the role of the emporium, *entrepôt* or relay was cut down to save transport and handling. Bordeaux began to send its sugar directly to Scandinavia from Saint Domingue without the necessity to weigh in at Amsterdam; Exeter and Hull their woollens to Cadiz, Lisbon and Hamburg, not to Amsterdam. Stockholm in the 20th century brought its wool directly from Australia, rather than London, and British re-exports shrank from 20-30 per cent of general imports in the 1780s to 15 per cent in 1910-1913.[1] Alfred Chandler found the same process of eliminating the middlemen to save handling and transport charges in the

1. ALBERT H. IMLAH, *Economic Elements in the Pax Britannica*, Cambridge, Mass.: Harvard University Press, 1958, pp. 205-207.

structure of American industry in the middle of the 19th century.[1] As an enterprise rose from the local to the regional to the national scale, distribution was taken back from wholesalers and jobbers and undertaken directly by the firm itself. In addition to the saving in handling charges, direct contact between seller and buyer permitted them to discuss possible improvements in the product, directly, without the filter of the intermediary merchant, and to understand each other better when it came to the producer instructing the buyer in product use, required in complex machinery and items such as chemicals that need precision in use. In today's terminology, this is the provision of software, which ends up, Sune Carlson suggests, leading the seller to design his own worldwide network of distribution the more effectively to instruct the consumer, to train service personnel in efficient maintenance, and to maintain depots of spare parts.[2]

Elimination of intermediary marketing steps has been a long drawn-out process in the application of the law of one price to trade, made economic as monopolies of information were diffused by direct contact, producing savings in transport and in communication about use. The same forces are not found in money and capital markets, which have tended to remain organized in more hierarchical form. The reasons are several. First, economies of scale are probably greater in trading money than trading commodities. Localities shift from net lenders to net borrowers and they converse more frequently and need a centralized market to minimize search costs. Secondly, costs of transporting money are far less than for goods so that the savings from shifting from indirect to direct trade are smaller. In combination these forces would argue for a single financial centre for a country or for the world. That solution, however, runs up against the need of financial institutions for credit information so detailed and up-to-date in a world of rapid change that it cannot be gathered, stored and maintained in a single centre given the present capacity

1. ALFRED D. CHANDLER, *Strategy and Structure. Chapters in the History of the Industrial Enterprise*, Cambridge, Mass.: M.I.T. Press, 1962.
2. SUNE CARLSON, 'Company Policies for International Expansion: The Swedish Experience', in TAMIR AGMON and CHARLES P. KINDLEBERGER, eds., *Multinationals from Small Countries*, Cambridge, Mass. and London: M.I.T. Press, 1977, pp. 49-71.

of computers. "Local knowledge" remains a critical adjunct of centralized statistics.

It is perhaps somewhat too strong to assert that savings in transport costs favour direct selling in traded goods, whereas search costs in borrowing or lending money favour a hierarchical organization of money flows where transport costs are negligible. For specialized lending, too many stages from one locality to a centre, across to another centre and down to a locality may filter out essential ingredients of the particulars of a problem. I once asked a banker in Aberdeen whether he got his information on oil-financing practices from Houston, Texas via New York and London or directly, and he said directly. Moreover in long-term lending, an initial underwriting syndicate need have no central location since structural costs of setting up the marketing group are overhead in character, met only once, and not repeated. These costs can be covered in underwriting commissions for the entire issue. In the present state of the art, however, the secondary market must have a single physical location to economize on the search costs of a buyer or seller who wants to trade one or at most a few bonds. It will take considerably greater cheapening of computer memories and distant communication to maintain bid and offer prices, and the location of the would-be traders, in one computer memory on a continuously changing basis reflecting data from the major and accessible money centres of the world.

6. The role of arbitrage

Segments of a given market are joined by arbitrage. Perhaps the most perfect market today in the absence of government interference is that for foreign exchange, where the costs of arbitrage are so low with cheap communication and a high level of competition that the market for a given currency, e.g., the dollar, is worldwide, and not confined to New York. In fact the market moves with the sun around the world each twenty-four hours from Western Europe, to New York, the West Coast, Singapore, Bahrein in the Middle East, and back next morning to Western Europe. At any moment of day or night it is possible to buy or sell millions of dollars somewhere. With adequate liquid funds in the hands of exchange dealers, moreover, spot and forward markets are joined so thoroughly as to make it a matter of indifference which market is used for trade, hedging, speculation, or, within credible limits, the defence of a currency by monetary authorities.

Arbitrage in precious metals and in money has built up slowly over time. As noted in our discussion of Gresham's law, gold-silver ratios could be maintained at disparate levels in different countries, within fairly wide limits, so long as costs of transporting specie were high. But more than freight is involved here. Freight costs move secularly down, but so do communication costs, which has made it possible for more and more people to scan wider horizons. The monopoly of merchants based on information meant that they alone looked for price differentials in order to buy cheap and sell dear, the engine that moves the law of one price. Banking specialists devised bills of exchange to substitute for specie in making payments at a distance, cleared them against one another in balanced trade to economize means of payment. Enormous rewards were available to the perspicacious observer who detected arbitrage opportunities where no one else did. Nathan Rothschild of the London house built his fortune to its preeminent scale by discovering that it was cheaper when Britain was paying the Duke of Wellington's armies and its Spanish allies in the Peninsula, Sicily and Malta for him to buy bills on bankers in those places in Paris, rather than have the paymasters in the field drawing bills on London that could be sold only at greater discounts. The monies to acquire French francs against sterling were obtained by selling gold in Paris. The French authorities countenanced the operation because they thought it would weaken Britain to lose gold.[1] The more usual joining of markets after rather than during wars gives opportunities to make profit in arbitraging foreign-exchange markets, as Keynes did, and gave rise to the purchasing-power-parity doctrine based on the notion that sufficient numbers of goods and services are arbitraged to keep price levels equated through the exchange rate. A number of modern theorists believe that arbitrage in goods is sufficiently perfect despite transport costs that the purchasing-power-parity theorem holds in the short run, as well as the long.[2] I do not. Non-traded goods and especially services, in my judgment, prevent the absolute version of the purchasing-power theorem from obtaining, but it would be futile to deny that the increased scope of the law of one price has been moving to greater perfection of goods arbitrage.

Financial markets are affected by changes in costs of transport and communications, as is true of trade, but the lesser importance of transport costs raises the importance in finance of changes in information leading to new horizons. Financial flows, like the international movement of labour in migration, take place for the most part in channels that connect particular markets, rather than smoothly over flat surfaces. New connections are made from time to time by some financial coup or success – the Baring loan, Thiers rente and Dawes loan are favourite examples of mine. British lending to France was halted after the Revolution of 1848 because of the outbreaks of xenophobic violence in that country which drove many skilled workers back to England, and killed some. The independence of the Spanish colonies in the 1820s

---

1. JOHN M. SHERWIG, *Guineas and Gunpowder. British Foreign Aid in the Wars with France, 1793-1814*, Cambridge, Mass.: Harvard University Press, 1969, pp. 328-9; Count EGON CAESAR CORTI, *The Rise of the House of Rothschild* (translated from the German by BRIAN and BEATRIX LUNN: *Der Aufstieg des Hauses Rothschild, 1770-1830*): New York: Blue Ribbon; London: Gollanz, 1928, pp. 114-19.

2. LAWRENCE H. OFFICER, 'The Purchasing-Power-Parity Theory of Exchange Rates: A. Review Article', *International Monetary Fund Staff Papers*, vol. XXIII, No. 1, March 1976, pp. 1-60.

led to a wave of British lending to South America. To stress these "displacements" is not to assert that investors are irrational, but primarily that they maximize returns within a given horizon, and that the horizon changes in response to discrete events. The horizon scanned by economic actors has been gradually enlarged, but limits remain as to how much information can be processed by individuals.

7. The problem of foreign direct investment

For the most part wider horizons increase the flow of factors, and of trade. In one particular respect, however, the wider horizons of producing firms may decrease trade, as production may take place for foreign markets abroad rather than at home, i.e. as wider knowledge and more information lead to foreign direct investment. Foreign direct investment can of course lead to more trade, rather than less.

The issue of the appropriate counterfactual – what would have happened if the direct investment had not taken place – is complex, of course. The exports might have declined in any event as the diffusion of monopolized technology on which comparative advantage rested meant that the comparative advantage was being lost through the normal workings of the product cycle. Moreover, some direct investment is undertaken to obtain inputs rather than to widen or to hold the market for outputs, and this enlarges trade.[1] The connection between trade and direct investment, too, is a factor extending the law of one price by widening the market. Horizons of firms have gradually increased through time to the point where today, major firms contemplate where next to invest by scanning opportunities virtually everywhere in the world.

If one ignores branches of banks and commission agents of merchants, which can be found in the Middle Ages, direct investment in manufacturing goes back to the middle of the 19th century, although significant investments on a substantial scale waited until the end of the 19th and beginning of the 20th centuries, and the burst of investment giving rise to the concept of the multinational corporation came after World War II.[2] Among the pioneers of the mid-19th century were several Britons

1. Gary C. Hufbauer and F. Michael Adler, *Overseas Manufacturing Investment and the Balance of Payments*, Tax Policy Research Study No. 1, Washington, D.C.: United States Treasury Department, 1968.
2. See Special Issue 'Multinational Enterprise', *Business History Review*, vol. xlviii, No. 3, Autumn 1974; Mira Wilkins, *The Emergence of Multinational Enterprise: American Business Abroad from the Colonial Era to 1914*, Cambridge, Mass.: Harvard University Press, 1970.

in the mechanical industries of Naples, as early as 1840,[1] the American Haviland in fine china in France in 1842,[2] the American Samuel Colt in firearms with interchangeable parts in 1852.[3] The German Siemens company was established in 1847 and by the early 1850s had a telegraphic equipment plant in Russia, by 1857 a submarine cable plant in Britain.[4] The real beginnings of the multinational corporation had to wait, however, until the steamship and especially the transcontinental jet aircraft. And the spurt of American investment in Europe was a response to a considerable degree to the Rome Treaty of 1957 establishing the Common Market, not because the Common Market created new profit opportunities, so much as the fact that it called attention to opportunities already in existence, acting, that is, as a displacement that extended the horizons of American businessmen and made them aware of missed chances.

1. LUIGI DE ROSA, *Iniziativa e capitale straniero nell'industria metalmeccanica del Mezzogiorno, 1840-1904*, Naples: Giannini Editore, 1968, Chapter 1.

2. CHARLES P. KINDLEBERGER, 'Origins of United States Direct Investment in France', *Business History Review*, Special Issue 'Multinational Enterprise', vol. XLVIII, No. 3, Autumn 1974, pp. 382-413, see p. 396.

3. MIRA WILKINS, *op. cit.*

4. JÜRGEN KOCKA, *Unternehmungsverwaltung und Angestelltenschaft am Beispiel SIEMENS*, Stuttgart: Ernst Klett Verlag, 1969, pp. 59-60.

8. The optimum economic area

In international monetary economics, Robert Mundell has put forward the concept of the optimum currency area, or that area which should have a single currency.[1] At the minimum, it would be a single person who might vary his subjective exchange rate with the rest of the world from day to day. At the maximum, the optimum currency area is the world. It is not relevant to our argument to discuss the various criteria put forward by Mundell and the economists who followed him to determine the optimum currency area (factor mobility, a discontinuity in trade between internal and external, the existence of institutions for determining policy). The present purpose is merely to broaden the optimum currency to the optimum economic area, and to suggest that it may differ for various goods and various social classes, varying inversely with costs of transport and of information. Since both of these are shrinking the optimum economic area is growing in size, and for many purposes is already at a world scale for the production and trade of goods.

However, economics is not the only consideration. The concept of optimum area can be extended to the political and social. These are presumably growing, along with the optimum economic area, but more slowly. The optimum social area is a function of the average citizen's sense of participation, of having a share in decisions, of counting. The unit as a whole must have a sense of cohesion, belonging, purpose. While the optimum economic area may be large, the optimum social area is clearly much smaller. There will be large countries that maintain cohesion and enlist the energies of their citizens in national purposes, and small ones that are divided on cultural, or other lines. A country like Belgium is evidently too small to constitute an optimum economic unit, but divided as it is between Flemish and Walloons, too large to constitute an optimum social unit. Moreover while the optimum scale of economic activity is getting larger and larger, the optimum social scale appears to be shrinking. Social and

1. ROBERT A. MUNDELL, 'A Theory of Optimum Currency Areas', *American Economic Review*, vol. LI, No. 4, September 1961, pp. 657-64.

political disintegration (Brittany in France, Wales and Scotland in Britain, Quebec in Canada) illustrates a tendency towards smaller units. The reaction against the multinational corporation implicit in works like Servan-Schreiber's *The American Challenge*[1] is a response to intrusion by foreign elements, fear that non-members of the group are making decisions affecting it, xenophobia which is perhaps innate in man in his primitive state. E. F. Schumacher's *Small is Beautiful*[2] purports to be an economic tract; it seems to me rather to be an expression of social reaction against the world market.

I have not reached any simple conclusion about the size of the optimum political unit, or its trend through time. The answer may turn on one's political objective function. If a country's purpose is to stay out of trouble, small is better than large although it is not riskless as the histories of Belgium, Holland, Denmark and Norway illustrate. If, on the other hand, a country is ambitious for glory, prestige, to leave footprints in the sands of history, bigger may be better. Prussia's Bismarck, Piedmont's Cavour, the United States' Theodore Roosevelt, perhaps France's de Gaulle point up this possible choice. The optimality function may be U-shaped, with payoffs to being small, without power or responsibility, or large and powerful with responsibility for world stability. What is awkward is the middle range, a country powerful enough to disturb political quiet, but too small to share naturally in world decision-making.[3] I suspect that the size of political units such as the European Economic Community is growing, but given the smallness of optimum social size, one cannot be sure.

Tension between economic and social size makes it difficult to say much about the future. First, it seems clear that progress (or perhaps I should use a less value-loaded word such as "change") will not be linear but uneven, with zigs intermingled with zags,

1. Jean-Jacques Servan-Schreiber, *The American Challenge*, New York: Atheneum, 1968.

2. E. F. Schumacher, *Small is Beautiful. A Study of Economics as if People Mattered*, New York: Harper & Row; London: Blond Briggs, 1973.

3. Charles P. Kindleberger, 'The International Monetary Politics of a Near-Great Power: two French episodes, 1926-1936 and 1960-1970', *Economic Notes* (Monte dei Paschi di Siena), vol. 1, Nos. 2-3, 1972, pp. 30-44.

and that there are occasions when it is necessary to *reculer pour mieux sauter*. Second, without being a Marxist, I believe it likely that in the long run economic factors will dominate the social. Tastes are already being homogenized around the world, with American plumbing, wall-to-wall carpeting and bland hotel decor being reproduced in multinationally-owned hotels in all but the most underdeveloped countries. I find it baffling that in the 19th century, the British and the French went separate ways, for example, in their taste as to what was appropriate to eat for breakfast – whether porridge, meat, eggs, toast and butter, and tea, or merely café-au-lait and a croissant. Today virtually all major national cuisines are available everywhere, and more and more resemble one another. On the supply side the world is much more homogeneous, of course, as technological diffusion has sped up since the early period when the industrial revolution of Britain was somewhat hesitatingly spread to the Continent.

A look at history emphasizes the dynamic path more than the trend. Keynes proved to be wrong when he urged 'National Self Sufficiency' to resist the law of one price in his famous *Yale Review* article of 1933.[1] But so was Bagehot, although his words were carefully hedged when he wrote in 1868:

A remarkable movement is going on in the world toward a uniformity of coinage between different nations. And it was begun in what seems the way of the nineteenth century; the way in which Germany was created, and the unity of Italy too; that is, not by a great number of states, of set design and in combination, chalking out something new but, on the contrary, by some great state acting first for its own convenience, and then other lesser and contiguous nations imitating its plan and falling in with its example. In this way France has now formed a great coinage league [The Latin Union] . . .

If things remain as now, she [Germany] is sure to adopt the French currency; already there is a proposal in the federal parliament that she should take it. Before long all Europe, save England, will have one money, and England be left outstanding with another money.

1. JOHN MAYNARD KEYNES, 'National Self-Sufficiency', *Yale Review*, vol. XXII, No. 4, June 1933, pp. 755-69; and also in *The New Statesman and Nation*, 8th and 15th July 1933; reprinted in *The Collected Writings of John Maynard Keynes*, vol. XXI, *Activities 1931-1939: World Crisis and Policies in Britain and America*, London: Macmillan, 1982, pp. 233-46.

This is a selfish reason for looking to our currency, but it is not the only reason. Every person must see that the demand for uniformity in currency is only one case of the growing demand for uniformity in matters between nations really similar. Many subjects, most subjects of legislation, vary between nation and nation; they depend on national association and peculiar idiosyncrasy and other causes. But commerce is everywhere identical; buying and selling, lending and borrowing, are alike the world over, and all matters concerning them ought universally to be alike too. In the old medieval 'law merchant' – the universal custom of trade which the international trader took with him from country to country – there was a recognition of a principle which we want now. The possession of special and very active legislatures by many states has broken up everywhere customary laws; the unity we need now must be a unity based on explicit treaty and voluntary agreements. But the idea is the same. Ultimately the world will see one *code de commerce*, and one money as the symbol of it.

And then comes the qualification:

We are, as yet, very distant from so perfect an age . . .[1]

Whether we are much nearer the one money today, 112 years after Bagehot wrote, as opposed to the one *code de commerce*, I hesitate to judge. My own view is that the force of the law of one price still pushes in that direction, but that the resistance at the social and political level will ultimately be overcome remains strong in the short and intermediate run.

Before concluding our analysis of the law of one price, it should be observed that in the field of money it calls for harmonization in the production of the public goods of monetary stability through appropriate monetary policies. I remain deeply disturbed by the monetary policy of 1971, when with fixed exchange rates and the New York and Frankfurt money markets joined through the Euro-dollar market, the American and German monetary authorities tried to go separate ways. It was impossible. In one money

---

1. WALTER BAGEHOT, 'A Universal Money' (*A Practical Plan for assimilating the English and American money, as a step towards a Universal Money*), London: Longmans 1869; reprinted in *The Collected Works of Walter Bagehot*, edited by NORMAN ST JOHN-STEVAS, London: The Economist, 1978, vol. XI, pp. 57-104, see 'Preface', pp. 64-6.

market, there is one rate of interest. The Federal Reserve System could not lower interest rates in pursuit of a boom to aid the re-election of President Nixon, at the same time that the Bundesbank undertook to raise interest rates to achieve price stability. One market and one price mean a joint policy on interest rates. The failure to recognize this simple and basic truth let loose a flood of dollars on the world and contributed seriously to the inflation of the 1970s, well before the rise in the price of oil in 1973.

9. Conclusions

I hope these four samples have been sufficient to indicate that the economic historian or historical economist who hopes to work on general-equilibrium problems must have many arrows in his quiver and not just one. If there had been time and endurance, one could have dealt with other powerful models or laws – the law of supply and demand, perhaps, although that is too general to tell us much, but the models of public vs private goods, property rights, the law of comparative advantage, the staple theory of growth of Harold Innes, Schumpeter on entrepreneurship, Marx on exploitation, world monetarism, many other powerful theories and models could have served as well. All, in my judgment, are partial, none is general. My theme remains that we must change from one tool to another as each serves the particular task in hand, and forgo any universal solvent or sovereign explanation.

Of course there must be specialization and exchange. Some economic historians work more with one tool than with another, just as medical specialists use some few tools more than others as they learn to penetrate the mysteries of various organs, to deal with babies or the aged, surgery or x-ray. But it is hubris for anyone to think that his speciality and his tool hold the key to the secret of life, just as I believe it is vain to think that one law or one model can unlock the basic secrets of economic history with their many dimensions in growth, technical change, adjustment, monetization and the like. Economists and economic historians should be like dentists, humble and with lots of tools.

DISCUSSION

CARLO DE CUGIS,[1] in using Keynes' analogy of economists as dentists referred to by Professor Kindleberger, identified four categories of 'dentists': (i) economists, who were supposed to treat *Homo oeconomicus*, but were often more interested in testing their own instruments, sometimes at the expense of their patients; (ii) economic historians, who attended to groups of historical men who, being dead, were unable to give an account of their symptoms; (iii) political economists who were interested in treatment for its own sake; and finally, (iv) historians of economic thought, who were the dentists' dentists because they treated the previous three categories.

Addressing the issue of tools, Professor De Cugis argued that economic historians, as well as using laws originally developed by economists, were beginning to formulate their own laws. In reference to the use of the economists' laws by economic historians, Professor De Cugis cited the English industrial revolution as an example of a unique event in economic history which, as such, could not be generalized by resorting to some economic law. Although the English industrial revolution was a complex phenomenon made up by various components (e.g. the increase in GNP and investment) which were amenable to being generalised by means of appropriate economic laws, yet the phenomenon itself consisted of a unique combination of interrelated processes. This called for an overall assessment aimed at answering questions such as whether or not the English industrial revolution had been a case of balanced growth.

Professor De Cugis, in alluding to the formulation of laws by economic historians, acknowledged that economic laws were relevant when historical events, however complex, were not unique. Industrialization, as a phase of growth, was a historical event that developed along the same lines for certain groups of countries according to the historical period in which it took place; thus one could classify industrializations by historical periods. This view was implicit in Marshall, who recognized that different historical agents tended to behave differently in different historical periods for given different initial conditions.

1. Professor of Economic History, Università degli Studi, Milano.

95

Professor De Cugis went on to describe how it was necessary to formulate empirical models with the same logical structure as the economists' universal laws, but with greater specificity of application. Unlike the economists' laws they would have to be relevant only to certain historical conditions and not applied to all places and periods. This explained why Hartwell had applied a model of 'balanced growth' to the English industrial revolution, while Gerschenkron had developed his 'big spurt' model for the processes of industrialization in continental Europe in the nineteenth century.

Finally, Professor De Cugis intimated that all economic historians would agree with Professor Kindleberger on the following points: (i) all economic laws should be tested against the events of economic history; (ii) no law intended to be of universal applicability was without substitutes for economic historical explanations; and (iii) economists and economic historians ought to switch from one law (or model) to another according to the economic event in question. However, Professor De Cugis wondered whether Professor Kindleberger would acknowledge that economic historians had the right to apply economic laws idiosyncratically, and to forge the tools of their trade.

Luigi Pasinetti[1] wishes to make a few remarks on what Professor Kindleberger has said in his lectures, from the viewpoint of a theoretical economist.

At the beginning of his first lecture, and then again at the end of his fourth lecture, Kindleberger made an important assertion, which has already been picked up and commented upon by Professor De Cugis. Kindleberger said – echoing a simile used by Keynes – that the idea of an economist he favoured is more like a dentist than a moral scientist. And a dentist – he pointed out – uses many tools: specific tools for specific purposes. Similarly, Kindleberger has made a plea for the use of many and diverse tools of economic analysis. Plurality of tools, rather than singularity of tools, seems to be Kindleberger's ideal.

On the face of it, the position seems irreproachable. Many are

1. Professor of Economic Analysis, Università Cattolica del Sacro Cuore, Milano.

always better than few: who could question that? Yet, if one goes deeper, one clearly has to specify and distinguish. For example, a marginalist economist would certainly like to have many tools of analysis, but within the logical framework of marginalist economics. He would be most unlikely to accept, let us say, Marxist analytical tools and concepts. The same – in reverse – would apply to a Marxist economist.

Thus, for a theorist, plurality of tools is all right, provided that this plurality is within a well defined theoretical framework. It cannot mean heterogeneity. The analytical tools may be many, but they cannot be logically incompatible with one another.

Yet, it is precisely on this point that Professor Pasinetti found Kindleberger's proposition most interesting. He is speaking from the point of view of the economic historian or, as he likes to put it, of the historical economist, or, more generally, from the point of view of the applied economist. And from this point of view it would appear that he is actually advocating heterogeneity, i.e. eclecticism.

In other words, Kindleberger is claiming that, for the theoretical economist, heterogeneity and eclecticism may well be a weak point but for the applied economist they are always a strong point.

This position has important theoretical implications. Professor Pasinetti would try to express what he meant by considering briefly some points relating to the first and the fourth of Kindleberger's lectures, that is, to Engel's law and the law of one price.

Engel's law is very simple, was presented towards the middle of the 19th century and is empirically extremely important.[1] The gist of it is that: 1) there is a hierarchy of consumers' wants; consumers satisfy first the most essential needs, and then – as income increases – they go on to satisfy other wants (to buy

---

1. GEORGE STIGLER pointed out in his article 'The Early History of Empirical Studies of Consumer Behavior', *Journal of Political Economy*, vol. 62, April 1954, pp. 95-113, that collection of data on the effect of income on consumer's demand began long before the development of modern consumer demand theory, while the collection of data on the effect of prices on consumer's demand did not start until *after* the development of modern consumer demand theory. This would seem to confirm that, empirically, the importance of changes in income – i.e. of Engel's law – is far greater than that of changes in prices in influencing consumption.

other, more sophisticated, goods); 2) wants become saturated so that, as income goes on increasing all the time, the increments of income expenditure will successively concentrate on different goods, or may sometimes go back to old goods, but considered in a different way and for different purposes (as Kindleberger has interestingly pointed out, with reference, for example, to second-car families). But the point is that the composition of the demand for consumer goods will change continually. These are essential features of human behaviour.

Now, although all applied economists and econometricians agree that all these tendencies represent a very basic empirical law, the prevalent theory of consumer behaviour has been unable to absorb it.

Three remarks on current theory were in order:

1. Today's consumer demand theory is a very sophisticated theory (which may be presented in many different guises; in terms of increments of expenditure *à la* Gossen, in terms of indifferences curves *à la* Pareto; in terms of revealed preferences *à la* Samuelson, etc.), but it is basically a theory that deals with problems of choice of consumers who are facing changing prices, at a *given* income. In such a context Engel's law is clearly irrelevant.

2. When utility functions are inserted into a growth model, they are always supposed to imply uniform elasticities of demand for all goods with respect to income. This is the precise negation of Engel's law.

3. Changing demand with increasing income means a changing structure of production and – what is more – of employment. What do the most well-known of the modern multi-sector growth models (the von Neumann model or the dynamic Leontief model) rely on? Proportional growth. *All* sectors are supposed to grow at exactly the same rate. Again this is a negation of Engel's law.

One may well understand now what Kindleberger means when he is pleading for heterogeneity of tools.

If one wants to analyse what historically is happening in a process of economic growth, where the structural dynamics of technology, production and consumption are the most conspicuous characteristics, of what use are prevalent consumer theory and current growth models? One would say very limited indeed.

There seems to be no choice but to go back to Engel's law. This may well be very simple, unsophisticated, even crude, but it is empirically relevant.

The lesson is clear: current theories are hopelessly deficient. No school of economic thought can claim today to have complete and systematic explanations of what is happening in economic systems. In these circumstances what can the applied economist do except pick up different, sometimes even contradictory, analytical tools at different times, for different purposes? If this is accepted, it should at least counsel, on the part of the theoretical economists, a little humility in their claims, and a patient tolerance of one another's views. Unfortunately, the prevalent attitude among economists today appears to be the opposite, namely one of arrogance and intolerance.

Professor Pasinetti had long been convinced of the crucial importance of the basic features of non-proportional growth in our economies and had been devoting a lot of efforts to a non-proportional multi-sector growth model in which technology, prices, production, consumption and employment all follow different movements through time, so as to characterize the economic system by a persistent and continuous structural dynamics.[1]

And he had been surprised by two things: 1) the breadth and depth of insights into historical economic development which even simple tools can provide, once proportional growth has been abandoned as a frame of reference; 2) the hostility, mistrust and suspicion that his economist colleagues instinctively showed towards the proposal of new analytical tools. When the tools that are proposed do not fit into the traditional mould, the reluctance to consider them is enormous. The excuses are innumerable: the model is "inelegant", it is "unrealistic" (an ob-

---

1. LUIGI PASINETTI, 'A New Theoretical Approach to the Problem of Economic Growth', *Pontificiæ Academiæ Scientiarum Scripta Varia*, no. 28, Vatican City, 1965, pp. 571-696; reprinted in *The Econometric Approach to Development Planning*, Amsterdam: North-Holland, 1965. See also *Structural Change and Economic Growth*, Cambridge: Cambridge University Press, 1981.

jection never made to traditional theory), it can be shown as a "particular" case of the old theory, and so on and so forth.

He was therefore pleased to find a historical economist, such as Kindleberger, pleading for new tools. He would like to consider this as an appeal for a more open attitude towards new, unconventional and, hopefully, more powerful, tools of economic analysis.

One further remark, on the law of one price. Kindleberger's emphasis has all been on the tendencies to equalization – in different places – of the prices for the same commodity. And, no doubt, the improvements in transportation and communication that have occurred in the past two centuries have favoured this tendency. On the other hand, he has not considered to the same extent what traditionally have been called the "factors of production".

In this field, especially with reference to labour, the tendency has not proceeded in the same direction. Whilst everyone is in favour of the mobility of goods, both government and public opinion resist the idea of mobility of people. It must not be forgotten that passports, visas and controls over the movement of people from one country to another are inventions of this century. And the differences in per-capita wages and per-capita incomes that may be observed today across countries all over the world are staggering. One might even claim they are unprecedented in history.

Here again no one of the prevalent theories can account for these differences. It is reasonable to infer that we need new analytical tools.

GIACOMO BECATTINI[1] said that Professor Kindleberger's lectures responded most admirably to a need that many in his audience, economists or historians, had certainly felt, namely, to define what concepts or economic tools were useful for training a historian and – more generally – what specific constructive contribution political economy could make to the job of unravelling the tangle of historical events.

1. Professor of Economics, Università degli Studi, Firenze.

His general message was clear and convincing.

According to Professor Kindleberger there was no single all-purpose theory or model that illuminated economic history. There was no single central theory that supplied all the answers.

The right approach was thus an eclectic one, picking one's tools with discrimination and making coordinated use of them. One would not easily forget the simile of the jeweller with his array of hammers, each with its slightly different task, a simile more appealing than the Keynesian one of the dentist with his drills. Given the state of the so-called science of economics, Professor Becattini fully agreed with this cautious and problem-oriented approach of Kindleberger. Naturally the problem of which tools to use – hammers, drills or pliers – in each particular case and in what order and in what way remained an open question. And here Professor Kindleberger offered help, specifying first four tools, Engel's law, the Marx-Lewis law, Gresham's law and the law of one price or Smith's law, as he had called it, and alluding to other, more or less well-known, tools, some belonging strictly to the field of economic analysis and others to social research more generally.

In a masterly exercise Kindleberger had shown how each of the four laws considered could be used as a key to read certain blocks of historical facts. Apparently unrelated and outwardly different events proved, in his telling reconstruction, to be closely interrelated or to be different examples of a single principle. In short, his four tools helped his audience to resolve the classic problem, so dear to Marshall, of detecting *the one in the many and the many in the one.*

Out of these four laws, one stood out as conceptually superior: Smith's law.

Professor Becattini's thesis was that it was like a Trojan horse within the group, which constituted a risk for Professor Kindleberger's adroit eclecticism. The view of the world that it embodied and that it mediated in the reading of historical events was heuristically so powerful that it forced every other tool of interpretation with which it was combined into a subordinate or coordinate role. It was more than a tool. It was, Professor Becattini submitted, the specific vehicle of a world view. If this was true, the simile of the tools lined up on the bench and used, separately and in succession, by the expert hand of the jeweller no longer held good.

Professor Becattini suggested to take a brief look at this law of Smith's. In a nutshell, it said that the reduction of the cost of transport in the broad sense of things, persons and ideas, by reducing the room for specialist intermediaries, had the effect – to use Professor Kindleberger's nicely-judged phrase – of making the world smaller. The engine of this contraction was the propensity that Kindleberger, taking up and rewording Adam Smith, believed to be deeply rooted in human nature, not only to buy and sell but *to buy cheap and sell dear*. The innate and unsuppressible urge to deal and make a profit on the one hand enlarged markets and on the other induced increasing specialization of labour and increasing technological and scientific progress, which in its turn enlarged markets and, by producing a sort of supermultiplier of trade, was enough on its own to account for the expansion of the economic universe. The paradigm was certainly no less convincing or heuristically valid and powerful than that of Ricardo and Marx, based on the withdrawal and subsequent accumulation of surplus value, and could also be coordinated with it. So Professor Becattini agreed on this key for reading the facts and on using it in a wide variety of historical contexts.

Where Professor Becattini began to feel uneasy was when Kindleberger seemed to embrace the thesis that this law of expanding trade and widening markets was necessarily accompanied by cultural standardization and down-levelling. The example of national cuisines getting so like one another that they were reduced to a distasteful or tasteless international hotchpotch had its point. Were this the principal effect of the law, it would end by running counter to the movement of goods and people and make not for growth but for stagnation, for the stunting of economic, social and cultural progress. Professor Becattini had taken Professor Kindleberger's culinary example but he could just as well have taken the example of language: whilst the advance of mass literacy and acculturation was on the one hand destroying – or putting at risk – "local" languages with their linguistic peculiarities, on the other hand it was enormously increasing the mass of participants in the "general talk", producing a wealth of new linguistic combinations. This line of reasoning applied to all goods and services, and to ideas too. The coming into contact on world markets of goods, services and ideas that had developed and matured in different cultures and then incorporated in other, sometimes very different, cultures did *not* produce *only* standardization and down-levelling *but also* and simultaneously hybridization and differentiation *ad infinitum*. Professor Becattini suggested this rather trivial example: "when I offer someone else a good, just as when I speak to him, I am absorbing *his* culture, I am projecting myself ideally into *his* cultural ground in order to understand his requirements and make them mine. If I do not, my offer is incomprehensible, meaningless". Trade, far from being a culturally empty or neutral fact, was a meeting point, an occasion for enrichment, for cultural mediation.

Professor Becattini wondered why this mediation should be thought of as leading only to levelling down. It was surely also the basis for greater articulation, differentiation and refinement of mankind's needs and tastes.

Bagehot's bizarre idea of a single coinage and a single *code de commerce*, referred to by Professor Kindleberger, seemed to be essentially bound up with the idea of an irresistible drive for growth of the capitalist mode of production which Marx himself at times incautiously accepted, or half-accepted! Hence the idea, taken up by Professor Kindleberger, that resistance to the law of one price, at social and political – or substantially suprastructural – level was destined in the long run to defeat: "My own view is that the force of the law of one price still pushes in that direction, but that the resistance at the social and political level will ultimately be overcome remains strong in the short and intermediate run".[1]

The idea that the "social and political level" produced only resistance and friction whilst the economic level alone engendered active and permanent forces seemed to Professor Becattini to be a pernicious legacy of the naturalistic and deterministic interpret-

---

1. See CHARLES P. KINDLEBERGER, *Lecture IV, The Law of One Price*, p. 90.

ation of social facts built into 19th-century economic thought: classical, neoclassical and Marxian deterministic.

This *de facto* surrender to economism was to Professor Becattini so odd and so incomprehensible in a thinker who had warned against "the universal solvent"[1] and who had cited among his recommended tools for the historian's training the Schumpeter of the entrepreneurial conception public goods vs. private goods models and other constructs clearly on the borderline between the economic and the social-political.

Professor Becattini very much admired the fascinating way in which Smith's law had been used by Professor Kindleberger to reduce a congeries of different phenomena to unity, but he was still convinced that it could only be accepted among the economist's tools after a thorough "ideological" verification.

CARLO FILIPPINI[2] raised two issues which, though expressed in the positive form, almost as certainties, actually concealed a series of questions, a request for elucidation.

His first remark concerned an application of Smith's law, the law of one price, namely the nexus between optimal economic area and scale of enterprise. Whilst he thought that the expansion of the market was certainly useful, he wondered whether the expansion of an enterprise had equally positive effects. He did not hold the view that small is beautiful, for various reasons, mainly because the term "small" is relative to a market and hard to define in the abstract. However, a case could be made for the view that the division of labour, which Smith related to the scale of the market and which he regarded as a growth factor, could be applied to enterprises as well as to workers. Specialization at enterprise level lowered unit costs and more medium-sized to small businesses were preferable to a few large ones. Professor Filippini claimed that the distinction between production unit and company was not always sufficiently clear. Conclusions pertaining to the former were often extended to the latter, and the costs of disseminating information and arriving at decisions in

1. See CHARLES P. KINDLEBERGER, *Lecture III Gresham's Law*, p. 44.
2. Professor of Economics, Università Commerciale "Luigi Bocconi", Milano.

complex organizations were underrated. Likewise, technological economies of scale were confused with financial or commercial economies of scale. An increase in the size of a production unit usually was called for because of objective needs for greater productivity whereas the increase in the size of a company depended, at times, on the desire to reduce uncertainty and to control the market more effectively, with results that did not come up to expectations. Professor Filippini remarked that from a theoretical standpoint the formation of oligopolies in a market eliminated the possibility of achieving a Pareto optimal solution and, as such, should be rated adversely.

His second remark was prompted by the historical references and syntheses between facts and theories that abounded in Professor Kindleberger's lectures and referred to the method used by economists in general. Professor Filippini observed that pithy terms were coined to give greater force to concepts that in themselves were to some extent open to question. The use of the word "law" was a typical example. Another well-known example was the use of the adjective "perverse" in connection with relations in capital theory. Economists had often tried to give their theories a scientific status by modelling them on other, established, sciences. This had meant a loss, on the one hand, of content in the attempt to defend only relations derived deductively on the model of mathematics and, on the other, of method in that only what was measurable on the model of physics was considered important and scientific. For this reason rigour had had the upper hand over relevance; as Robert Gordon said,[1] maximum rigour had often been sought without relevance instead of maximum relevance with the rigour that was possible. In effect, scientific rigour did not depend on quantification, on measurement, but on a clear and precise process of data collection and examination, of formulation of explanatory hypotheses and of verification of the latter according to the method of deductive-inductive hypothesis. This *per se* involved no need whatever to quantify all concepts.

1. ROBERT A. GORDON, 'Rigor and Relevance in a Changing Institutional Setting', *American Economic Review*, vol. 66, No. 1, March 1976, pp. 1-14.

Admittedly, measurement had been necessary in order to counter the numerous objections that have been raised regarding the possibility of science in the field of human action, that is the possibility of putting the human sciences on an objective footing. Professor Filippini felt that it was a matter of defining a given discipline and its rules of falsification. Of the various objections one, not the most important, was worth remembering: the fact that in the human sciences there were no deterministic relationships but the action of the free will of the human being, one of whose characteristics is thought to be the possibility of choice, would make it difficult, if not impossible, to generalize or predict, since past actions may not be repeated in the future. However, human sciences study collective, average and not individual specific behaviour. Moreover, more importantly, it was all due to a shortcoming of economists, to their reluctance to get away from "precise" methods instead of taking a closer look at the social context. It was due, in other words, to the temptation to stick to the safe and incontrovertible and avoid chancing one's arm in research that, in many respects, may appear unscientific. The outcome of this attitude was a sort of abstraction in many economic analyses, a kind of disregard of the social picture that was so important in explaining some economic relations.

Bruno Jossa[1] addressed his remarks to the second lecture given by Professor Kindleberger, the one dealing with the iron law of wages or the Lewis model of growth. Professor Kindleberger had made wide use of this model, with great erudition and intelligence, in many of his writings; and to many the Lewis model had always seemed extremely interesting. Professor Jossa prefaced his remarks by expressing his full agreement regarding economic-historical interpretations of the type Professor Kindleberger had made, which focused attention on this type of model.

The Lewis model was – in a few words – a model with unlimited supplies of labour and hence a model with constant or slowly rising wage rates; and it was a model in which saving was kept going mainly by profits but also by rent and so it was a model in

---

1. Professor of Economics, Università degli Studi, Napoli.

which capital and income grew at a rising rate. All this applied to the first phase of economic growth, that is as long as there was an unlimited supply of labour. But in the course of this phase, capital was accumulated very fast and so, full employment of labour would result eventually. In passing, it should be noted that in the second phase these conditions no longer held good.

In this model many hypotheses and relations were undoubtedly classical in approach but Professor Jossa would not go so far as to call it the Lewis-Marx model as some had done. Professor Kindleberger himself had said that the Lewis model "has a strong family resemblance to Karl Marx's model of growth" and it was this statement of his that prompted Professor Jossa to take issue with him on some points. The model assumed that in the initial period there was heavy unemployment and unlimited supplies of labour and showed by what routes rapid accumulation would eventually produce full employment; a sweeping generalization that Professor Jossa found unacceptable.

Professor Jossa recalled that the model had been formulated for the first time in the mid-1950s and stemmed from the idea that in the less developed countries, for which it had been originally conceived, there would always be "at the outset" a large supply of "hidden unemployment". In those years an investigator of the stature of Myrdal had maintained in one of his books that the hidden unemployment in underdeveloped countries was around 30 per cent of manpower, a real army of unemployed.[1] But of course opinion on this point had since changed considerably.

Professor Jossa merely wished to express doubts and not to pit one view against another. But to make his argument more effective he would, just for a moment, pit one view against another and recall the opinion of authoritative Marxist economists, according to whom in precapitalist systems there was usually full employment and that it was in the course of capitalist development that capital tended to save on manpower and that widespread unemployment was generated for long periods. In this

1. GUNNAR MYRDAL, *An International Economy. Problems and Prospects*, London: Macmillan; New York: Harper, 1956, p. 193.

view, since for Marxists socialism was the system that ensured full employment, things would go in exactly the opposite way to what the Lewis-Kindleberger law suggested: capitalism would be "a parenthesis" in man's history, a parenthesis characterized by continuing and widespread unemployment.

But one should go cautiously here, because the Lewis model was an interesting one and Kindleberger's interpretation so penetrating that one could not go so far as to suggest replacing it with a world view opposite to the one implicit in the model. But what could be said was that very often, and not episodically, unemployment *was created* by capitalist development and not eliminated by it, partly because capitalist development destroyed precapitalist systems, destroyed artisan activity and small businesses because of the enormous shift of population away from agriculture into industry, and because, especially for latecomer countries, technical progress steadily destroyed jobs. The Italian case strongly suggested that when in the course of capitalist development there was a population shift from agriculture to the towns the employment rate could well fall for years on end (because women especially could no longer find work).

These were, of course, old ideas. The argument that capitalism by its very nature destroyed precapitalist activity and hence a host of jobs in handicrafts, small-scale trade and so on, was the very idea that Marx argued very well in his days in a series of articles in an American newspaper of the time, the *New York Daily Tribune*. But even recently a writer like Giovanni Arrighi,[1] studying Rhodesia, showed that capitalist growth in that country did not start from a surplus labour situation to reach a labour shortage situation but rather the reverse.

Professor Jossa then pointed to Italy – the striking feature of the Italian case, which all students of Italy's economic development had discussed, was the big drop in the rate of participation of the labour force. And this fall in employment suggested that economic development in some way reduced job opportunities

1. See GIOVANNI ARRIGHI, 'Labor Supplies in Historical Perspective: A Study of Proletarization of the African Peasantry in Rhodesia', in GIOVANNI ARRIGHI and JOHN S. SAUL, eds., *Essays on the Political Economy of Africa*, New York and London: Monthly Review Press, 1973, pp. 180-236.

and induced many to leave the labour market so that they would not even figure among the unemployed. Professor Jossa recalled as his last point the fact that in Italy there had been a great deal of discussion (especially by journalists, in brilliant contributions) as to whether accumulation was the independent variable and consequently wages the dependent variable, as Marx said in *Das Kapital*,[1] or whether the reverse was the case and wages were the independent and accumulation the dependent variable (as Marx himself seemed to admit in *Wages, Price and Profit* and as researchers of the Bank of Italy under Governor Carli had said many times). It was not easy to find agreement on this issue but the point in the study of the labour market in Italy on which a consensus did exist was that the demand for labour *generated* its supply and so the labour supply was somehow, to some extent obviously, a *dependent* variable. If this was true, then it would be a powerful argument against the Lewis model.

As evidence of the fact that the labour supply was a dependent variable and that the size and growth of the population were not crucial to an increase in the labour supply Professor Jossa mentioned the lowering of retirement age, the raising of school-leaving age and other similar measures, which reduced the labour supply significantly, for there was reason to believe that economic policy measures or social tendencies that generally reduced the supply of labour were the *consequence* of a scant demand for labour. Professor Jossa wondered whether this meant that capitalism often created (especially for latecomers) so few jobs that on occasion many had to be induced to quit the labour force.

To conclude, in Professor Jossa's view, for many latecomers like Italy, it was often the case that in the course of capital accumulation, in the course of the most rapid phases of industrialization and during crises, the imitation of the most advanced techniques of advanced countries, which were highly *labour-saving* techniques, the imitation of the living standards of the advanced countries, which led to high wages, and the limited growth of

---

1. See KARL MARX, *Capital: A Critique of Political Economy* (transl. by BEN FOWKES, with an Introduction by ERNEST MANDEL), vol. 1, Harmondsworth: Penguin, 1976, Chapter XXIII.

the tertiary sector (these and other causes taken together) meant that this type of economic development, far from always creating jobs, destroyed them. The key to an understanding of the Italian case was thus slightly different from the model that should rightly be called the Lewis-Kindleberger model.

ANGELO PORTA's[1] remarks referred to the lecture on Gresham's law and in particular to what Professor Kindleberger had said about the possibility of analysing the phenomenon of crises by making use of the broadest version of the law, which was not confined, to remain within the strictly monetary field, to the problems raised by the coexistence of good and bad money but, broadening its scope, envisaged a wide range of alternatives to money.

In making his remarks Professor Porta said that he would try to keep to the spirit that informed the lectures, which Professor Kindleberger had so aptly summed up in the introduction to his first lecture when, quoting Donald McCloskey, he had reminded his audience that economic history should serve to produce, among other things, better economic theory and better economic policy.

Professor Kindleberger also had emphasized that he was an historical economist, not an economic historian. Professor Porta said as he was neither he should perhaps apologize in advance for poaching on other people's territory.

Professor Porta said that he would confine himself to two points, one on economic policy and the other on economic theory, and that in neither case he would consider the international implications.

As to economic policy, the lesson that emerged from the interpretation of history that Professor Kindleberger had given through Gresham's law was that financial instability was always latent. Financial systems were not always and necessarily unstable, but financial crises could arise rapidly and history showed that they did.

1. Associate Professor of Economics, Università Commerciale "Luigi Bocconi", Milano.

This lesson of history was, perhaps, not sufficiently heeded in the period of intense development that followed the Second World War. The economic policy authorities' attitude to the financial structures, which in the 1930s had been designed to increase their stability, underwent a gradual shift of emphasis. In the growth years the stability of the financial structures fell into the background and the authorities directed their efforts chiefly to increasing the efficiency of the credit institutions and improving their function as transmitters of the impulse of short term monetary policy. This change of attitude was reflected in the various reforms of credit systems undertaken in several countries towards the end of the 1950s and even more in the 1960s, reforms whose purpose was to increase the competitiveness and efficiency of the structures, removing in numerous cases many of the restrictions dictated by the previous preoccupation with stability. In the 1970s events brought financial instability, which seemed to be only a memory in previous decades, back to centre stage. In recent years the leading industrial countries had seen a wave of financial reforms, prompted in the first place by concern about instability, and a rekindling of the argument about the most appropriate form of intervention to safeguard financial stability.

From this preface, Professor Porta asked his first question. Professor Kindleberger had expressed in his lectures and more explicitly elsewhere, that is, in his recent book on financial crises,[1] a preference for safeguarding stability by strengthening the role of the monetary authorities as lender of last resort not only at an international but also at a domestic level. Professor Porta surmised that it would be interesting to know what Professor Kindleberger thought about other approaches that had taken shape in recent years in discussions on financial stability, especially what he thought about the view that the authorities should not intervene unduly in order to avoid crises at all costs. Those who had taken this line had argued that intervention by the authorities could have adverse effects because, if the system was sure that

---

1. CHARLES P. KINDLEBERGER, *Manias, Panics and Crashes. A History of Financial Crises*, London: Macmillan; New York: Basic Books, 1978.

the authorities would intervene, the stimulus to a correct and nonspeculative conduct on the part of credit institutions would be weakened. In this connection Professor Porta asked for Professor Kindleberger's view on alternative modes of safeguarding stability, such as those based on a wider use of insurance (insurance on deposits, for instance), and on the strengthening of the capital base of credit institutions, modes that had been discussed at length latterly.

Turning to theory, Professor Porta took his cue from Professor Kindleberger's statement that a monetary theory that had no room for the instability of Gresham's law could not be regarded as complete, on which he agreed. However, when considering the history of thought, it had to be acknowledged that monetary theory, or at any rate what constituted orthodoxy in the long period preceding Keynes' work, had not attached undue importance to instability. As Hicks pointed out when discussing Ricardo's monetary theory,[1] the existence of financial instability was quite clear to economists, for whom it was a fact of daily life. Instability was written about extensively in applied economics and, said Hicks, was kept well in mind by bankers but normally received scant attention from pure economics. This attitude could certainly not be attributed to all the pre-Keynesian economists but it was fairly general. Hicks found it in Ricardo and another economist who had this attitude to a more marked degree than others was Walras, who throughout his life was constantly concerned with monetary themes, and on several occasions joined in debates on the monetary questions of his day and wrote many essays on them.[2] So Walras was well aware of the existence of financial instability but when he turned in the various editions of the *Elements* to developing his pure theory of money, he completely put aside the problem of instability and worked out a monetary theory in which it had no place. The pure theory of money with its abstract models and monetary history, so full of episodes of instability, thus seemed for long to have led

1. JOHN R. HICKS, 'Monetary Theory and History: An Attempt at Perspective', in *Critical Essays in Monetary Theory*, Oxford: Clarendon Press, 1967.

2. His main monetary essays are collected in *Etudes d'économie politique appliquée*, Paris: Pichon, 1898.

separate lives. According to Hicks, this separation could be traced back to the fact that the basic concern of the majority of pre-Keynesian theorists was to construct a theory that would explain the long-term evolution of economic systems and the method used for this analysis left no room for financial instability. Professor Porta felt that it would be very interesting to know Professor Kindleberger's opinion of this interpretation of Hicks and, more generally, on the problems raised by the separation, which had often been very marked, between monetary theory and monetary history.

Professor Porta made one last brief remark on the subject of theory. According to him Keynes's analysis of money in the *General Theory* took ample account of Gresham's instability. Indeed the demand for money for speculative purposes fitted into a context in which instability and the uncertainty of expectations were of great moment. It was therefore very odd that Keynesian monetary theory, which seemed to rest on an attentive consideration of financial instability,[1] should have ended by generating an economic policy which, as Professor Kindleberger himself had pointed out in his third lecture, attached so little importance to instability. This was another point on which Professor Porta wished to hear Professor Kindleberger's opinion.

PIETRO MANES[2] argued that Professor Kindleberger's treatment of Gresham's law provided further support to his own view that what was needed was not a new currency to replace all others but rather, quite paradoxically, a currency *to be replaced* by all others. Such a currency, explained Professor Manes, would only perform the task of a universally accepted store of value, and not that of sole and universal means of payment. According to Gresham's law, it would thus be driven out of circulation and jealously guarded in the vaults of central banks. This currency should not be a credit instrument but rather a non-

---

1. The importance of financial instability in Keynes has recently received considerable attention in the process of reinterpretation of the work of Keynes. Very interesting remarks in this connection are to be found in HYMAN MINSKY, *John Maynard Keynes*, New York: Cambridge University Press, 1975.

2. Economic Adviser, R.A.S., Riunione Adriatica di Sicurtà, Milano.

interest bearing physical commodity such as gold. Special Drawing Rights did not fulfil this requirement and merely provided further scope for currency speculation.

Addressing Professor Pasinetti's remark that international differences in wage rates contradicted the law of one price as stated by Professor Kindleberger, Professor Manes pointed out that one of the fundamental errors of non-Marxian political economy was to regard labour just like any other commodity. In the aggregate accounts of a given economy, suggested Professor Manes, the cost of labour was an income item, a component of the economy's aggregate output. This, perhaps, could explain why differences in labour costs could not be regarded as contradicting the law of one price.

FABRIZIO ONIDA[1] found Professor Kindleberger's definition of integration as a trend towards factor-price equalization rather unilluminating. Both Samuelson's theorem of factor-price equalization and the law of one price held good on the very assumptions that modern theories of international trade were trying to make redundant.

Professor Onida's criticisms referred to three problems: defining a factor unit; the definition of a competitive market; and the shape of production functions.

As to the definition of factor units, Professor Onida recalled that Leontief himself, in an effort to explain his own paradox, had suggested that a labour unit in the United States was quite different from a labour unit in Europe. The same could be said, added Professor Onida, of other countries and of capital units.

On his second point, Professor Onida recalled that modern competition theories emphasized that markets were not perfectly competitive; that there were various barriers to entry; and that there was no equal access to product- and process-innovations.

With reference to the shape of production functions he pointed out that they were not necessarily linear (especially in view of the uneven distribution of managerial skills).

1. Professor of International Economics, Università Commerciale "Luigi Bocconi", Milano.

Professor Onida submitted that in order to gain a better understanding of economic integration in today's world far greater
emphasis should be given to the diffusion of technology, the dissemination of tastes, and the changes in the patterns of saving and
financing investment. In all these three respects an explanation
of how economic integration overcame political boundaries, and
geographical distance, could be afforded by examining multinational enterprises and international movements of physical
and human capital, which, added Professor Onida, had been the
subject-matter of some recent excellent papers by Professor
Kindleberger himself.

FRANCESCO SILVA[1] wondered whether the four laws so masterly
described in Professor Kindleberger's lectures were compatible
with each other. More precisely, Professor Silva made the point
that the law of one price was not consistent with both Engel's
law and the iron law of wages, in so far as the former implied
value-judgments and a world-view which were incompatible
with the latter's.

Professor Silva recalled that Engel's law was a dynamic theory
which envisaged demand as a function of income (taken as the
independent variable). However, as Professor Kindleberger had
pointed out, it was also a forerunner of product-cycle theories
and helped to explain both the pattern of industrial growth and
the international division of labour. Any dynamic firm (or
country) on the growth frontier had to move on the S-curve
identified by Professor Kindleberger in order to earn monopoly
profits which were the Schumpeterian mainspring of growth.
Firms had to enter the market on the upward part of the curve
and to diversify production on its downward part. The final
limb of the S-curve, where the law of one price was indeed applicable, was left to the late-comers. These had an advantage to
specialize in old products because of favourable relative prices
of the factors of production, especially labour. However, in so far
as productivity was the main determinant of the long-term trend

1. Professor of Economics (Microeconomics), Università Commerciale "Luigi Bocconi", Milano.

of wages (as shown by some recent work by Professor Turner), this advantage was short-lived. This was because the use of imported technology brought about a rapid rise in productivity and, albeit with a lag, in wages. Thus even late-comers had to find more favourable points on the product-cycle in order to earn monopoly profits and avoid a slow-down in growth. Engel's law, therefore, explained why a growth-oriented firm (or country) had to avoid falling into the very phase of product life to which the law of one price did apply.

As to the iron law of wages, Professor Silva believed that for it to be consistent with Engel's law either or both of the following conditions had to hold: (i) an unequal domestic distribution of income; and (ii) growth of exports. Both these conditions held in Italy in the 1950s and 1960s; thus the Lewis-Kindleberger and Engel models could coexist and explain jointly the twenty-year period of growth in Italy during those two decades. Professor Silva was not sure whether the Lewis-Kindleberger law was compatible with the law of one price. Growth resulted from differences in factor-prices, especially the price of labour; when such differences disappeared, explained Professor Silva, growth could be sustained only by innovating and diversifying, thereby escaping the law of one price. Thus, concluded Professor Silva, if the law of one price held good, the laws that accounted for growth did not. Professor Silva felt that his remarks could be seen as a roundabout way of expressing a widespread belief. This belief was that there existed a wide gap between the theories of market equilibrium and efficient resource allocation (as summed up in the law of one price) on the one hand, and growth theories (such as Engel's and Lewis' laws) on the other.

GIOVANNI BELLONE[1] referring to Professor Kindleberger's first lecture, and precisely to his suggested extensions of Engel's law beyond food, did not know whether such extensions were validated by empirical evidence. Professor Kindleberger had not provided such evidence.

However, Professor Bellone wished to make a different point.

1. Professor of Economics, Università degli Studi, Padova.

Any extension of Engel's law beyond food and shelter would alter radically the basic message of the law itself. He interpreted Engel's law as simply saying: when income is low patterns of consumption are very compelling, and if income increases they become less compelling.

Indeed in empirical estimates of Engel's law one saw that heteroscedasticity increased with increasing income. Of course it would be possible to correct automatically for heteroscedasticity by adopting appropriate forms of Engel functions (as in general had been done),[1] but the correction was based on the assumption that, by the very nature of the phenomenon, the variance of the error term is different across observations.

In conclusion Professor Bellone wished to point out that when the extensions of Engel's law suggested by Professor Kindleberger were taken into consideration, one further good was implicitly added, that is "discretionary behaviour" or, to use a more important word, "freedom from want".

GIULIANO MUSSATI[2] wondered whether Gresham's law could be used to explain the instability of industrial growth in recent periods if it were extended beyond financial assets and some real assets (e.g. real estate and land) to include both tangible assets such as capital goods and intangible ones such as know-how and goodwill. Such an extension, argued Professor Mussati, could help to explain the extent to which changing expectations with respect to the yields on alternative assets could account for both a lower propensity to invest and the switch to financial and low-risk real assets (e.g. real estate and land).

To the extent that multinationals and industrial policy-makers considered both the decision to switch from one product-cycle curve to another and the possibility of affecting the rate of

1. See e.g. CONRAD EMMANUEL VICTOR LESER, 'Forms of Engel Functions', *Econometrica*, vol. 31, October 1963, pp. 693-703; HENDRIK S. HOUTHAKKER, 'An International Comparison of Household Expenditure Patterns, Commemorating the Centenary of Engel's Law', *Econometrica*, vol. 25, October 1957, pp. 532-51; HENDRIK S. HOUTHAKKER, 'New Evidence on Demand Elasticities', *Econometrica*, vol. 31, April 1965, pp. 277-88.

2. Lecturer in Industrial Economics and Policy, Università Commerciale "Luigi Bocconi", Milano.

growth of demand for a given product as strategic choice variables, it could be argued that the very structure of markets could be affected by the active policies pursued by industrial policy authorities and large enterprises (e.g. R&D policies, technology transfers, product diversification). In Professor Mussati's view, the increasing importance of these phenomena since the 1960s could account for the increased instability in the patterns of growth. In fact, the uncertainty surrounding technology transfers, the competitive behaviour of large firms, and the industrial policies pursued by national agencies, could all affect the uncertainty regarding the trends of the variables determining the returns on alternative productive activities, thereby favouring a switch to financial and low-risk real assets in accordance with a generalized version of Gresham's law.

COMMENTS
by Charles P. Kindleberger

Professor Kindleberger found himself overwhelmed by the number and variety of interesting points made in the discussion by the several speakers, and regretted that, because of the brief time allotted, he could not do justice to many of them. He decided to offer a few comments, nonetheless, following the subject-matter in order of the lectures, rather than of the speakers, leaving to the end the methodological point addressed by many.

To a certain extent he felt that he might safely back away from any participation in the debate by pointing out how many comments in one direction had been counterbalanced by others from a diametrically-opposed viewpoint, although it had to be acknowledged that central positions were not on that account correct, but could be merely half as wrong as others. As to Engel's law, he observed that while PROFESSOR BELLONE was unhappy about the generalization about food and shelter to all items of consumption, a number of others – PROFESSORS PASINETTI, SILVA and MUSSATI – seemed to be willing to accept this idea. He himself quite agreed with Professor Bellone. If the law were to be stretched beyond food and shelter, then something had to remain a luxury, with an income elasticity greater than one (if only savings, or in a somewhat paradoxical fashion, non-income, or leisure). However, Professor Kindleberger maintained that diminishing returns in consumption of specific items of expenditure, such as were involved in the product cycle so interestingly tied to early and late entry by PROFESSOR SILVA, had to be acknowledged as a fact of life. Professor Kindleberger warned that the income elasticity of a given good – for instance, a television set, car, bicycle, or whatever – would differ depending upon whether it were the first, second, third. . . . in the household, so that the average income elasticity for all television sets constituted a mish-mash dependent on income distribution. However, he believed that it could not be denied that Engel's law, or diminishing returns in consumption, was a pervasive and powerful influence in economic development and growth.

Professor Kindleberger remarked that PROFESSOR PASINETTI's interest in non-proportionality in growth models was surely welcome. It was understandable that economic theorists preferred to focus on balanced growth in which all factors, demands for all goods, technological progress, and the like all grew at a constant rate, because the mathematics was easier, much in the way of the familiar story of the man who lost his ring at point A in the dark, but looked for it at point B because the light was better. In this respect, Professor Kindleberger welcomed the abandonment of such empty exercises as golden paths as a positive development for the economics profession.

Professor Kindleberger then turned to the comments prompted by his second lecture on the Lewis model or the iron law of wages. PROFESSOR JOSSA'S objection seemed to rest on a view of Karl Marx that there had been no unemployment or underemployment before capitalism. Professor Kindleberger was not sure whether this proposition had to be taken as a theoretical construct or as a fact. It was widely accepted that Engels' view of the happy cottage textile worker with his children playing around him as he worked a few hours a day before being forced into the 12 to 14 hour day of the factory was romantic nonsense. Professor Kindleberger recalled that there were even Keynesians who claimed that there had never been any unemployment before the First World War because wages had been compressible downward prior to the depression of 1920-21. Any more than cursory acquaintance with the historical literature would dispel these notions, commented Professor Kindleberger.

Professor Kindleberger accepted that the introduction of mechanized methods of production destroyed old manual methods and wreaked havoc with cottage industry unable to make the transition, as was illustrated by Indian, Irish, and Silesian textile industries. This was capitalism. It was also a universal result of production methods under any system; those who could not adapt suffered. Professor Kindleberger put himself with those who thought that technological unemployment was real and tragic for individuals, but manageable as a social problem with appropriate policies. As to the failure of Italian employment to increase Professor Kindleberger referred to the explanation provided by economists such as Professor Giorgio Fuà who had emphasized the duality of the Italian labour market with much employment in the smaller firms of the south remaining unreported. However, he claimed no expertise in this field.

PROFESSOR SILVA had been kind enough to link Engel's law and the iron law of wages to the law of one price, all contributing equally and together to the problem of efficient resource allocation, whereas PROFESSOR BECATTINI believed that the law of one price dominated the others. PROFESSOR MUSSATI had gone one step further in suggesting that Engel's law with high growth rates produced by the iron law of wages of Sir Arthur Lewis and the shrinking world of the law of one price could even give rise to instability of the Gresham's-law type, if the latter were extended beyond monies, and money vs. other financial assets, to all financial vs. real assets. Professor Kindleberger felt that these excursions were much more daring than he had chosen to be in treating these laws as equal *and separate*, nevertheless he found these ideas worth pursuing.

Professor Kindleberger believed that Gresham's law stood a little to the side of the other three laws or models since it dealt with disequilibrium rather than equilibrium situations. PROFESSOR PORTA had raised three critical issues in this respect, one each of theory, fact and policy. The theoretical point dealt with the exegesis of Keynes' *General Theory* which had been taken by most later Keynesians to be an equilibrium theory, but by Minsky and Porta to emphasize increasing strain in debt positions that led to instability. The historical question was how to explain the stability of the twenty years or so after the Second World War after 400 years of financial crises which followed each other more or less at 10 year intervals. With regard to policy, Professor Porta had asked whether such instability as existed would not be best treated by leaving it alone, since knowledge by credit institutions that they would be cared for in trouble made them more careless and likely to get into trouble.

In Professor Kindleberger's judgment these were good and important questions. In his view the *General Theory* had ample room for instability, but the exegesists had put stability in, reducing it to geometry and a system of equations. Moreover, the historical fact of extensive stability after the Second World War probably rested on the growth of government as a built-in stabilizer, albeit at some cost in inflation. On the issue of policy, there was clearly a dilemma, as in the case of moral hazard in insurance. A typical outcome was to dissemble: to promise not to intervene to stiffen the responsibility of credit institutions and make them more careful, but then when they got into trouble, to intervene, thereby preventing the contagion of deflation spreading. That ethically unsatisfactory devil was only a temporary one, of course, since after a time the protests of non-intervention were no longer credible.

Professor Kindleberger doubted whether he would be completely understood the thrust of PROFESSOR MANES's interesting suggestion that what was needed was not one money to replace all others, but one money to be replaced by all others. Gresham's law referred to money as a medium of exchange and store of value. He agreed with Professor Manes as to the need for one dominant money as a unit of account. Some years ago the most successful economist in world history, Professor and President Luigi Einaudi, wrote about "imaginary" money being needed in Milan because there were some 50 different coinages circulating in the city in the eighteenth century, which could only be handled by equating them separately to an abstract unit of account.[1] However, Professor Kindleberger was not sure that he agreed if Professor Manes had in mind the store-of-value function as seemed implicit in his reference to gold.

Finally Professor Kindleberger turned to the law of one price where again various participants in the debate had taken different sides in the argument. PROFESSOR PASINETTI thought that the law of one price applied in actuality to goods but not to factors, and Professor Manes had taken him to task for treating labour as a commodity. Professor Kindleberger accepted that there was a so-called gap between wages in developed and developing countries, especially as economic growth proceeded in the former, although this was partly between countries that had, and those that had not, passed through the Malthusian demo-

1. LUIGI EINAUDI, 'Teoria della moneta immaginaria nel tempo da Carlomagno alla Rivoluzione francese,' *Rivista di Storia Economica*, 1936, vol. I, pp. 1-35; translated by GIORGIO TAGLIACOZZO as 'The Theory of Imaginary Money from Charlemagne to the French Revolution', in FREDERICK CHAPIN LANE and JELLE C. RIEMERSMA, (eds.), *Enterprise and Secular Change. Readings in Economic History*, vol. III Homewood, Ill.: Irwin, 1953, pp. 229-61.

graphic revolution. Within the developed world, however, there had been a considerable equalization of both wages and interest rates.

PROFESSOR ONIDA wanted to reject the price-equalization theorem altogether on the grounds that there existed no such factors as labour and capital – units of labour incorporated varying amounts of human capital so that it was not possible to get a meaningful total by merely counting heads; physical capital's productivity was tied up with managerial capacity; markets were uncompetitive; and production functions were nonlinear. Professor Kindleberger found these arguments powerful; however, he was puzzled by PROFESSOR ONIDA's contention that the multinational corporation was a strong force for world integration as it spread technology, managerial ability and moved capital. In Professor Kindleberger's view there was a paradox here. In a recent paper, Niehans had concluded that the multinational corporation could be seen as vertical integration across national boundaries undertaken for fear of the market, fear of being cut off from inputs on the one hand, or from markets for outputs on the other.[1] To the extent that markets did not work and multinational corporations substituted for them, the law of one price might still operate even with some adulteration of monopoly pricing. The remarks of PROFESSOR FILIPPINI were germane here, particularly the distinction between the efficient size of production units and the most profitable size of company in oligopolistic markets.

Among the comments on his fourth lecture, Professor Kindleberger found particularly interesting PROFESSOR BECATTINI's unhappiness at his suggestion that the optimum economic and the optimum social size were at war with one another. Also of interest was Professor Becattini's claim that trade and travel spread cultural enrichment rather than dilute separate cultures by homogenizing them. Professor Kindleberger hoped that Professor Becattini was right, and that the optimum social unit

---

1. JÜRG NIEHANS, 'Benefits of Multinational Firms for a Small Parent Economy: The Case of Switzerland,' in TAMIR AGMON and CHARLES P. KINDLEBERGER, eds., *Multinationals from Small Countries*, Cambridge, Mass.: M.I.T. Press, 1977, pp. 1-39.

was congruent with the optimum economic one. However, spreading neo-mercantilism, resistance to immigration, social and economic discrimination against minorities made Professor Kindleberger think the clash was a real one. Nationalism was sometimes said to be a collective good like a public park. In the years ahead it would appear many times that social units resisted the movement to economic integration of markets for goods and factors. In the long run, he thought it hopeless to sustain this resistance, just as the dream of the anthropologist of preserving unique cultures had proven to be utopian.

Professor Kindleberger wished to conclude by addressing the comments on methodology, and particularly the insightful comments of PROFESSORS FILIPPINI, BECATTINI, PASINETTI and DE CUGIS. He could not help feeling pleased that so many preferred his metaphor of the silver smith's hammers to Keynes' more vivid and sensitive one about dentistry.

PROFESSOR FILIPPINI had raised the age-old questions about rigour and relevance. The choice, or the twisting path, between them was vital for economic policy. It was even more relevant when it came to history. Models or laws that sought to explain large events of history could be elegant, but their explanatory power was likely to be limited. The insistence that one had to choose between induction and deduction was of course based on illusion. Knowledge came from endless leapfrogging back and forth, dealing with facts and with their theoretical formulation.

PROFESSOR BECATTINI's dictum that the four tools were one, according to Marshall's motto of the 'one in the many and the many in the one', was a stimulating idea. Professor Kindleberger felt that his own message was that one always learnt from dis-aggregation, and that economists were better at partial-equilibrium than at general-equilibrium analysis, and were more insightful when they served as specialized economists than as moral philosophers.

He supported PROFESSOR PASINETTI's plea that no economist should use all the possible tools or tricks of the trade. If economists had to believe anything at all, we had to believe in specialization, exchange, and comparative advantage within their trading area. However, marginalist economists had to admit that they would be less well off in autarky, and that they benefited from importing other economic specialities.

Finally, Professor Kindleberger turned to PROFESSOR DE CUGIS' interesting and pointed questions on whether models were not superior to laws, whether economic history should be concerned with general processes or with unique outcomes, and whether there was not a need for a general theory of growth, if not *à la* Rostow, then according to the insights of Hartwell and Gerschenkron. Professor Kindleberger found PROFESSOR DE CUGIS' arguments forceful, but was unwilling to recant, and forbore from repeating what he had said. He surmised that they had arrived at the real distinction between the economic historian and the historical economists, with both of them rather straddling the divide, not cleanly on one side or the other. The economic historian was more interested in outcomes whereas the historical economist was beguiled by economic processes. On this issue de Cugis and Kindleberger conformed to their avowed vocations. However, continued Professor Kindleberger, interest in laws was more historical while models were theoretical, thus they reversed positions on this issue. As to whether growth conformed to historical economics or economic history, Professor Kindleberger had no inner conviction, but returned to the belief that one could use the laws he had paraded before those present to explain various salient aspects of the growth process, though he was still unwilling to accept one of the big grand theories. It was those over-arching, all-encompassing, mono-causal structures that he fundamentally opposed.

BIOGRAPHY
of Charles P. Kindleberger

1. Biographical Note

The name Kindleberger is originally Swiss, from the valleys near Berne and was borne by landless peasants who went among great numbers to the Palatinate in Germany, my ancestors perhaps in the early eighteenth century, to make a living in the mercenary armies of the Elector of Hesse. A Kindleberger came to the American colonies in the middle of the eighteenth century, originally to Philadelphia, with its rim of villages with such names as Germantown, King of Prussia and the like. One of them moved with many other Germans to Ohio where my grandfather, David Kindleberger, was born in 1835. Where his father was born I do not know, but he was named Thomas Jefferson Kindleberger so that he was probably born about 1800.

David Kindleberger went to college in Ohio, became a doctor, joined the United States Navy. He married the daughter of another naval officer, Charles Poor, my greatgrandfather who had been born in 1803 in Cambridge, Massachusetts. I am named after Charles Poor Kindleberger, their first son, who like his father became a medical doctor in the navy. My father, E. Crosby Kindleberger, was born in Washington, D.C. on one of his father's tours of duty there. He became a lawyer with offices in New York City.

My mother, Elizabeth Randall McIlvaine Kindleberger, was born in Annapolis where her mother's family, the Randalls, lived. She grew up in Philadelphia, where her father, Henry C. McIlvaine, was in the wholesale drug business.

I was born in New York, in the borough of Manhattan, on 12th October 1910 and lived there for almost a decade with four sisters (no brother). In 1919, the family moved to Flushing, N.Y., then an attractive suburb. I started schooling in New York City and Flushing, but at 14 years went to Kent School in Kent, Connecticut, from which I was graduated in 1928.

From Kent I went to the University of Pennsylvania which my father and uncle had attended in the 1890s, perhaps the peak of alumni loyalty to one's university. My initial field of concentration was in classics, Latin and Greek, but at the end of the second year I switched into economics, ostensibly because of a pedantic and disagreeable teacher in Horace, doubtless in reality because my interests were changing as the 1929 depression deepened. The 1930s attracted many people into economics, motivated by curiosity and a desire to understand why the system was breaking down.

Although the depression made the study of economics interesting, it did not help to finance it. My father's law practice was hard hit, and I was unable to win one of the very few fellowships available for graduate study in economics at the time. Through pure luck, I was offered financing at Columbia University by the alumni of a social fraternity there that was in danger of collapse and needed a few more bodies to establish a critical mass. They offered to pay my way to law school, but had no objection when I chose economics instead. The opportunity came in the fall of 1933, after I had worked a year as an office boy in a firm of marine-insurance brokers.

Graduate education in economics at Columbia suffered several drawbacks in those years, but we were fortunate enough to benefit from one-year transfers from the University of Chicago of Milton Friedman and W. Allen Wallis, from regular visits of Rockefeller fellows from Europe who included Fritz Machlup, Michael Heilperin, E. A. Radice, E. F. Schumacher. The biggest stimulus for me was the arrival at Columbia from Cambridge University in England, in 1935, of H. H. Villard, who had attended Keynes' seminar for a year. This was before the *General Theory* actually appeared, but not before it had generated great excitement. In 1936, Villard and I organized an informal seminar that met in the apartment of Arthur R. and Evelyn Burns. Those meetings were as stimulating as any organized instruction. One meeting helped me get a job at the Federal Reserve Bank of New York, when W. Randolph Burgess attended and arranged an interview for me at the Bank of which he was vice president.

My original interest was in foreign-exchange questions and international economics generally. This had been stimulated by working on ocean-going ships during summer vacations from college – through the Panama Canal to the West Coast in 1929, and to Copenhagen, Gydnia, Helsingfors and Leningrad on a freighter in 1930. In 1931, moreover, I was fortunate enough to win a scholarship for the summer to the Graduate School of International Studies at Geneva, Switzerland, directed by Sir Alfred Zimmern. My first published paper, written as a graduate student and appearing in the *Harvard Business Review*, dealt with competitive exchange depreciation between Denmark and New Zealand as they struggled to dominate the London butter market in the early 1930s.[1] In 1937 I completed my doctoral dissertation on international short-term capital movements which dealt with the similarities and differences between gold and foreign-exchange reserves in the balance of payments on the one hand, and in domestic monetary arrangements on the other.[2]

The 1930s were a poor time to get an academic job. In fact, I do not recall that I contemplated applying for a job in a college or university. Instead, I wanted to understand the foreign-exchange market. The job at the Federal Reserve Bank of New York did not open up right away, and I spent the summer of 1936, before having completed my dissertation, in the United States Treasury Department, working with Frank Coe, under Harry Dexter White, on purchasing-power-parity calculations for the French franc which was devalued in the fall. After three months, I switched to the New York Bank, working half-time in the Foreign Research Department on British problems, and half-time in the Foreign Department in a small section on foreign exchange, with Emile Despres.

In the spring of 1937 I was married to Sarah Bache Miles, born in Princeton, New Jersey, and grown in Baltimore, where her father, Professor L. Wardlaw Miles, taught English at Johns Hopkins University. Over the following twelve years we had four children: Charles P. Kindleberger 3rd, now a city planner in St. Louis, Missouri; Richard S. Kindleberger, a journalist in Boston, Massachusetts; Sarah Kindleberger, a teacher of autistic children in Boston; Elizabeth Randall Kindleberger Rosen, an assistant professor of French history at the University of Maine

---

1. 'Competitive Currency Depreciation between Denmark and New Zealand,' *Harvard Business Review*, vol. XII, No. 4, July 1934, pp. 416-27.

2. *International Short-Term Capital Movements*, New York: Columbia University Press, 1937; reprinted in Reprints of Economic Classics, New York: Augustus M. Kelley, 1965.

at Machias. They have produced five grandchildren for my wife and me.

After two and a half years at the Federal Reserve Bank of New York, I changed jobs to work for the Bank of International Settlements in Basle, Switzerland, under the Bank's economist, Per Jacobsson, having made the decision to go in February 1939 before the German invasion of Czechoslovakia. The move proved to have been a mistake as the outbreak of war cancelled the monthly meetings of central bankers which provided much of the interest of the position.

When Paris fell in June 1940, Despres, who had transferred to the research staff at the Federal Reserve Board in Washington, arranged a job in the international section for me there. The Board was called upon to provide bodies for the American side of the Joint Economic Committee of Canada and the United States. Alvin Hansen on leave from Harvard University to the Board was made the American Chairman; I became the secretary. We worked on joint Canadian-American issues of wartime cooperation, but these quickly were taken over by the agencies involved with direct dealing between the two sides and no need for intermediation. In the spring of 1942, the Committee turned exclusively to postwar problems. Given the state of the war, these lacked immediacy. Accordingly when Emile Despres invited me to join him again, this time in the Office of Strategic Services (O.S.S.), I did so, in the summer of 1942.

The Office of Strategic Services, that later developed into the Central Intelligence Agency, had one major division, the Research and Analysis Branch (R and A), consisting of academic social scientists – historians, geographers, political scientists and economists. R and A was headed by a Board of Analysts on which the economists were Edward S. Mason and Emile Despres. Under the Board there was, among others, an economics division headed by Chandler Morse, with several sections – on industrial production, manpower, agriculture, and war material – devoted to estimating enemy economic activity. I was in charge of the section on material.

In the fall of 1942, R and A set up an Enemy Objectives Unit in the Economic Warfare Division of the United States Embassy in London, to assist the strategic air forces of the United States in selecting target systems and individual plants within systems for aerial bombing attack. Chandler Morse, Walt W. Rostow and William A. Salant made up the initial contingent of the Office of Strategic Services men in E.O.U. In February 1943 I changed places with Morse as head of the unit.

In the spring of 1944 we were asked by the strategic air forces to help them plan an optimal strategy for heavy bomber support of the invasion of France. In May and June, I was assigned on temporary duty with the tactical airforces during the invasion, still concerned with how best to attack enemy supply and transport. In July 1944, I transferred altogether to the G-2 staff of 12th Army Group, commanded by General Omar N. Bradley, to provide intelligence to assist the ground forces in making the most effective use of their associated tactical air forces. In due course, I was joined in this work by, among others, Robert V. Roosa.

Having been overseas from February 1943 to June 1945, with one brief respite, I was anxious after V.E Day to get home. Despres again came to the rescue. Many members of the the Office of Strategic Services staff had transferred into the Department of State to work on such postwar problems as German reparations. I made it back to Washington by 12th June 1945, and after a week's leave was busy in the Department of State backstopping the reparations work at Moscow and Potsdam. That fall I tried to switch out of occupation issues, and worked briefly on the British loan with Undersecretary of State for Economic Affairs, William L. Clayton. German problems remained exigent, however, and soon I was back among them as chief of the Division of German and Austrian Economic affairs, along with Rostow, William Salant, Harold J. Barnett and others of the Office of Strategic Services days. This continued until June 1947 when the Secretary of State, George C. Marshall, broached a European-wide recovery plan. I moved into that work in the Department as an advisor.

The years from 1942 to 1948 were full of hard work, with a one-week vacation in 1945, none in 1946 or 1947. In 1948 I had an operation, lost weight, and decided to quit government for an academic job. Invitations to give seminars at Princeton and Yale turned out badly, as I defended the Marshall plan against the views of Friederich Lutz, Frank D. Graham and Jacob Viner, who believed that the European balance of payments could have been corrected with exchange depreciation and restrictive macroeconomic policies. Finally Richard Bissell who had been the chief staff member on the Harriman report analysing the impact of the Marshall plan on the United States economy, told me of an opening in international economics at Massachusetts Institute of Technology. I applied, visited the campus, was not asked to give a seminar, which may have been fortunate, and got the job.

My first research at M.I.T. was an attempt to justify the necessity for the Marshall plan in a book entitled *The Dollar Shortage*.[1] This appeared in 1950. A few years later when dollars seemed more than plentiful, I came in for a great deal of teasing about the title. With hindsight, it is clear that the book should have been given a title something like "persistent balance-of-payments disequilibrium". Many economists find equilibrium in virtually all markets. I seem to have taken a different position early, insofar as balances of payments are concerned, and later in studying financial crises, especially international ones.

The textbooks that I wrote in the early fifties were efforts at self-education to make up for the 12-year absence from the academy. I revised one four times and the other once, before turning them over to younger collaborators. As explained in "The Life of an Economist",[2] my interest in economic history grew out of a moonlighting course on "The Economy of Europe", taught at Columbia University. Fairly fresh from the State Department work on the Marshall plan, I was primed for the contemporary portion of the course in the second term, but weak on the historical background that made up the bulk of the first term. In the course of making up this deficiency, I stumbled on the very different tariff histories of Britain, France, Germany, Italy and

---

1. *The Dollar Shortage*, Cambridge, Mass.: Technology Press of M.I.T.; New York: John Wiley & Sons; London: Chapman & Hall, 1950.
2. 'The Life of An Economist', *Banca Nazionale del Lavoro Quarterly Review*, No. 134, September 1980, pp. 231-45.

Denmark, responding to the dramatic fall in the price of wheat after 1879, and wrote "Group Behavior and International Trade",[1] seeking to explain the differences in response in models that went beyond the set usually found in international trade, and edging into sociology. Comparative economic history, or perhaps more accurately, comparative historical economics has interested me ever since. A monograph compares economic growth in France and Britain.[2] "Group behavior . . ." and a series of other papers are collected in *Economic Response. Comparative Studies in Trade, Finance, and Growth*.[3]

Interest in foreign exchange, balances of payments, international capital movements and international monetary arrangements has persisted from graduate-student days. *Europe and the Dollar*[4] and *International Money. A collection of essays*[5] both bring together papers on these related subjects. Among the most noteworthy, perhaps, are 'Measuring Equilibrium in the Balance of Payments', which appeared in the *Journal of Political Economy*[6] in 1969, and, with two close friends, Emile Despres and Walter S. Salant, 'The Dollar and World Liquidity: A minority view', in *The Economist* for 5th February 1966,[7] both reprinted in *International Money*. Both emphasize that some countries serve as bankers to the rest of the world, others like clients of banks, and that their balances of payments should be viewed differently, as should their policies with regard to exchange rates and other macro-economic variables.

A persistent belief in fixed exchange rates as a first-best policy runs through these essays – a continuation of early ideas. It stems from a belief in the efficiency of money. Flexible exchange

1. *Journal of Political Economy*, vol. LIX, No. 1, February 1951, pp. 30-46.
2. *Economic Growth in France and Britain, 1851-1950*, Cambridge, Mass.: Harvard University Press; London: Oxford University Press, 1964.
3. Cambridge, Mass. and London: Harvard University Press, 1978.
4. Cambridge, Mass. and London: M.I.T. Press, 1966.
5. London: George Allen & Unwin, 1981.
6. Journal of Political Economy, vol. 77, No. 6, November-December 1969, pp. 873-91; reprinted in *International Money. A collection of essays*, London: George Allan & Unwin, 1981, pp. 120-38.
7. *The Economist*, vol. CCXVIII, No. 6389, 5th February 1966, pp. 526-29; reprinted, in the original version, in *International Money, op. cit.*, pp. 42-52.

rates are the antithesis of international money, usually defined as the only asset fixed in price in terms of itself. There is a price to be paid for the benefits of international money (i.e. fixed exchange rates), and the world may be unwilling to pay it. Many economists, however, have erred in my judgment in deeming flexible exchange rates a first-best system, by analogy with flexible prices for goods in partial equilibrium. Because of its pervasive effects, however, the exchange rate cannot be analyzed in partial-equilibrium terms.

I suppose I could be regarded intellectually as a grasshopper who moves from problem to problem, gets a limited amount of mileage out of each one by the use of intuition, with limited statistics, no econometrics, and minimal formal analysis. One such topic that I have touched on on several occasions is the multinational corporation. A brilliant student, Stephen H. Hymer, made a breakthrough in this field in his dissertation of 1960,[1] but had difficulty initially in exploiting it. Using and perhaps marginally extending his insight, I have produced one set of lectures, have another collection of papers in press, and have edited several symposia in the field.

Finally, interest in disequilibrium and in economic history are combined in *The World in Depression, 1929-1939,*[2] in *Manias, Panics, and Crashes. A History of Financial Crises,*[3] and to a considerable degree in *A Financial History of Western Europe.*[4]

Luck is important to research, and not only in stumbling on useful books that one did not know about as one searches a library shelf for something else. I was asked to write a book on foreign trade in various economies after the untimely death of the first choice. That resulted in *Foreign Trade and the National Economy.*[5] Wolfram Fischer of the Free University of Berlin, the editor of a series on world economic history by decades, published orig-

1. Stephen H. Hymer, *The International Operations of National Firms: A Study of Direct Foreign Investment,* Ph.D. thesis, Massachusetts Institute of Technology, 1960, published Cambridge, Mass.: M.I.T. Press, 1976.

2. Berkeley, Cal.: University of California Press; London: Allen Lane, The Penguin Press, 1973; Second edition, 1986.

3. London: Macmillan; New York: Basic Books, 1978.

4. London: George Allen & Unwin, 1984.

5. New Haven and London: Yale University Press, 1962.

inally by Deutsche Taschenbuch Verlag, first asked Alexander Gerschenkron to write one in the series, and when Gerschenkron declined, asked me, offering me a choice of decades. Rather arbitrarily I picked the 1930s. I finished the manuscript in 1971, not at all prescient in forecasting the depression years of 1974-1975 or 1979-1982. That book led naturally to *Manias Panics, and Crashes*,[1] again apparently foreseeing the international debt crisis of 1982-1983, but mainly written in 1977.

Sitzfleisch, as the Germans say, is critical to research. So is luck.[2]

1. *Manias, Panics and Crashes. A History of Financial Crises*, London: Macmillan; New York: Basic Books, 1978.

2. Charles P. Kindleberger's AFFILIATIONS: American Economic Association, Nominating Committee, 1951; Board of Editors, *American Economic Review*, 1956-1958; Executive Committee, 1961-1963, Vice President, 1966, President-elect, 1984.

Royal Economic Society; Economic History Association; Economic History Society; American Academy of Arts and Sciences.

HONORS: D. h.c. University of Paris, 1966; D. h.c. University of Ghent, 1971; presented with a book, JAGDISH BHAGWATI, RONALD W. JONES, ROBERT MUNDELL, and JAROSLAV VANEK, eds., *Trade, Balance of Payments and Growth*, Papers in International Economics in Honor of Charles P. Kindleberger, Amsterdam and London: North-Holland, 1971.

Harms Prize, Institut für Weltwirtschaft, University of Kiel, 1978; Distinguished Fellow, American Economic Association, 1980.

OTHER SERVICE: Occasional consultant to Board of Governors of the Federal Reserve System, Federal Reserve Bank of New York, U. S. Treasury Department, The International Bank for Reconstruction and Development (the World Bank).

Trustee and Trustee Emeritus, Clark College, Atlanta, Georgia; Member, President's Advisory Committee on International Monetary Arrangements, 1965-1966; Chairman, M.I.T. Faculty, 1965-1967.

2. Bibliography

'Competitive Currency Depreciation between Denmark and New Zealand', *Harvard Business Review*, vol. XII, No. 4, July 1934, pp. 416-27.

'The Theory of Inflation and Foreign Trade', in H. Parker WILLIS and John M. CHAPMAN, eds., *The Economics of Inflation. The Basis of Contemporary American Monetary Policy*, New York: Columbia University Press, 1935, pp. 371-8.

International Short-Term Capital Movements, New York: Columbia University Press, 1937; reprinted in Reprints of Economic Classics, New York: Augustus M. Kelley, 1965.

'Flexibility of Demand in International Trade Theory', *Quarterly Journal of Economics*, vol. LI, No. 2, February 1937, pp. 352-61.

'Speculation and Forward Exchange', *Journal of Political Economy*, vol. XLVII, No. 2, April 1939, pp. 163-81.

'The Economic Tasks of the Postwar World' (with Alvin H. HANSEN), *Foreign Affairs*, vol. 20, No. 3, April 1942, pp. 466-76.

'International Monetary Stabilization', in Seymour E. HARRIS, ed., *Postwar Economic Problems*, New York: Books for Libraries Press, 1943, pp. 375-98.

'Planning for Foreign Investment', Papers and Proceedings of the Fifth-fifth Annual Meeting of the American Economic Association (Washington, D.C., January 1943), *American Economic Review*, vol. XXXIII, No. 1, Supplement, Part 2, March 1943, pp. 347-54.

'Interim Report on the Rail Movement of German Reserves' (June 16, 1944), in Walt W. ROSTOW, ed., *Pre-Invasion Bombing Strategy*, Austin, Tx: University of Texas Press, 1981, Appendix F, pp. 122-37.

'Memorandum from E. G. Collado to Mr Clayton: "United States Foreign Policy towards Europe and its Economic Implications"' (February 25, 1946), in Walt W. Rostow, ed., *The Division of Europe after World War II: 1946*, Austin, Tx: University of Texas Press, 1981, pp. 102-4.

'Memorandum for the Files: Origins of the Marshall Plan', (July 22 1948), in *Foreign Relations of the United States, 1947*, vol. III, Washington, D.C.: United States Government Printing Office, 1972, pp. 241-7.

'The Foreign-Trade Multiplier, Propensity to Import and Balance-of-Payments Equilibrium', *American Economic Review*, vol. XXXIX, No. 2, March 1949, pp. 491-3.

'Germany and the Economic Recovery of Europe', *Proceedings of the Academy of Political Science*, A Series of Addresses and Papers presented at the semi-annual Meeting of the Academy of Political Science (April 7, 1949) on 'The United States and the Atlantic Community', vol. XXIII, No. 3, May 1949, pp. 68-81.

The Dollar Shortage, Cambridge, Mass.: Technology Press of M.I.T.; New York: John Wiley & Sons; London: Chapman & Hall, 1950.

'International Disequilibrium', *Canadian Journal of Economics and Political Science*, vol. 16, No. 4, November 1950, pp. 529-37.

'Bretton Woods Reappraised', *International Organization*, vol. V, No. 1, February 1951, pp. 32-47.

'Group Behavior and International Trade', *Journal of Political Economy*, vol. LIX, No. 1 February 1951, pp. 30-46.

'European Economic Integration', in *Money, Trade, and Economic Growth*. In honor of John Henry Williams, New York: Macmillan, 1951, pp. 58-75.

'The Mechanism for Adjustment in International Payments – The Lessons of Postwar Experience' (with Emile Despres), Papers and Proceedings of the Sixty-fourth Annual Meeting of the American Economic Association (Boston, Mass. December 26-29, 1951) *American Economic Review*, vol. XLII, No. 2, May 1952, pp. 332-44.

International Economics, Homewood, Ill.: Richard D. Irwin, 1953; Second and revised edition, 1958; Third edition, 1963; Fourth edition, 1968; Fifth edition, 1973; Sixth and Seventh editions with Peter LINDERT, 1978 and 1982.

'L'asymétrie de la balance des paiements', *Revue Économique*, vol. V, No. 2, Mars 1954, pp. 166-89.

'German Terms of Trade by Commodity Classes and Areas', *Review of Economics and Statistics*, vol. XXXVI, No. 2, May 1954, pp. 167-74.

'Anciens et nouveaux produits dans le commerce international', *Économie Appliquée*, vol. VII, No. 3, Juillet-Septembre 1954, pp. 281-97.

'Les termes d'échange de la Belgique entre 1870 et 1952', *Bulletin d'information et de documentation*, vol. II, No. 3, September 1954, pp. 1-10.

'The Position and Prospects of Sterling', *Journal of Political Economy*, vol. LXIII, No. 1, February 1955, pp. 70-3.

'Industrial Europe's Terms of Trade on Current Account, 1870-1953', *Economic Journal*, vol. LXV, No. 1, March 1955, pp. 19-35.

'Economists in International Organizations', *International Organization*, vol. IX, No. 3, August 1955, pp. 338-52.

Statement on 'The Regional Approach to United States Foreign Policy', in *Foreign Economic Policy*, Hearings before the Subcommittee on Foreign Economic Policy of the Joint Committee on the Economic Report, Congress of the United States, 84th Congress, First Session, Washington, D.C.: United States Government Printing Office, 1955, pp. 509-40.

The Terms of Trade: A European Case Study, (with the assistance of Hermann G. VAN DER TAK and Jaroslav VANEK), Cambridge, Mass.: Technology Press; New York: John Wiley & Sons; London: Chapman and Hall, 1956.

'Tariff Policy in the United States – A Strong Rich Country', Proceedings of the American Farm Economic Association, *Journal of Farm Economics*, vol. XXXVIII, No. 2, May 1956, pp. 309-15.

'Aspects sociaux de la formation de capital dans les pays sous-developpés', *Cahiers de l'Institut de Science Économique Appliquée*, Serie F, No. 3, 'Niveaux de développement et politiques de croissance', 10, Juin 1956, pp. 35-51.

'Partial – vs. General-Equilibrium in International Trade', *Indian Journal of Economics*, vol. XXXVIII, No. 148, July 1957, pp. 31-8.

'Une surabondance de modèles des fluctuations cycliques internationales', *Revue Économique*, vol. VIII, No. 6, 'Les récessions economiques', Novembre 1957, pp. 927-38.

'Imports, the Tariff and the Need for Adjustment', in *Foreign Trade Policy*, A Compendium of Papers presented to the Subcommittee on Foreign Economic Policy of the House Committee on Ways and Means, 85th Congress, Washington, D.C.: United States Government Printing Office, December 1957, pp. 73-87.

Economic Development, New York: McGraw-Hill, First edition 1958; Second edition 1965, Third and Fourth editions with Bruce HERRICK, 1977 and 1983.

'The Terms of Trade and Economic Development', Papers, and Abstracts of Papers, presented at a Conference on International

Economics called by the Universities-National Bureau Committee for Economic Research, *Review of Economics and Statistics*, vol. XL, No. 1, Part 2, Supplement, February 1958, pp. 72-85.

'The Dollar Shortage Re-Revisited', *American Economic Review*, vol. XLVIII, No. 3, June 1958, pp. 388-95.

'New Trade Channels', *Challenge*, vol. 7, No. 5, February 1959, pp. 64-9.

Statement on 'Employment, Growth, and Price Levels', Hearings before the Joint Economic Committee, Congress of the United States, 86th Congress, First session, (June 29, 30, July 1 and 2, 1959); Part 5: *International influences on the American Economy*; Washington, D.C.: United States Government Printing Office, 1959, pp. 954-8.

'United States Economic Foreign Policy: Research Requirements for 1965', *World Politics*, vol. XI, No. 4, July 1959, pp. 588-613.

Statement on 'Implications for the U.S. Resulting from Gold Outflow', Hearings before the Joint Economic Committee, Congress of the United States, 86th Congress (July 16, 1959): *The Commercial Chronicle*; Washington, D.C.: United States Government Printing Office, vol. 190, No. 5864 (July 16, 1959), pp. 1, 30-2.

'International Political Theory from Outside', in William T.R. Fox, ed., *Theoretical Aspects of International Relations*, Notre Dame, Indiana: University of Notre Dame Press, 1959, pp. 69-82.

'The Technical Basis of Economic Integration', *World Politics*, vol. XII, No. 3, April 1960, pp. 462-7.

'The Comparative Statics of United States Foreign Trade – United States Commercial Policy', in Ralph E. FREEMAN, ed., *Postwar Economic Trends in the United States*, New York: Harper & Brothers, 1960, pp. 339-73.

'La fin du rôle dominant des États-Unis et l'avenir d'une politique économique mondiale', *Cahiers de l'Institut de Science Économique Appliquée*, No. 113, Série P, No. 5, Mai 1961, pp. 91-105.

Statement on 'The Problem of World Liquidity and Payments', Hearings before the Subcommittee on International Exchange and Payments of the Joint Economic Committee, Congress of the United States: *International Payments Imbalances and Need for Strengthening International Financial Arrangements*, (May 16, June 19, 20, and 21, 1961), Washington, D.C.: United States Government Printing Office, 1961, pp. 283-5.

'Obsolescence and Technical Change', *Bullettin of the Oxford University Institute of Statistics*, vol. 23, No. 3, August 1961, pp. 281-97.

'Foreign Trade and Economic Growth: Lessons from Britain and France, 1850 to 1913', *Economic History Review*, Second series, vol. xiv, No. 2, December 1961, pp. 289-305; reprinted in James D. THEBERGE, ed., *Economics of Trade and Development*, New York-London-Sydney-Toronto: John Wiley and Sons, 1968, pp. 46-66; also reprinted in Malcom E. FALKUS, ed., *Readings in the History of Economic Growth*, Nairobi-Lusaka-New York-London: Oxford University Press, 1968, pp. 135-53.

'International Trade and Investment and Resource Use in Economic Growth', in Joseph J. SPENGLER, ed., *Natural Resources and Economic Growth*, Washington, D.C.: Resources for the Future, 1961, pp. 151-90.

Foreign Trade and the National Economy, New Haven and London: Yale University Press, 1962.

'Tariff Reductions to Correct Balance-of-Payments Difficulties', *Industrial Management Review*, vol. 3, No. 2, Spring 1962, pp. 1-7.

'Protected Markets and Economic Growth', in *Factors Affecting the United States Balance of Payments*, Compilation of Studies prepared for the Subcommittee on International Exchange and Payments of the Joint Economic Committee, Congress of the United States, 87th Congress, Second session, Washington, D.C.: United States Government Printing Office, 1962, pp. 157-73.

'Foreign Trade and Growth: Lessons from British Experience since 1913', *Lloyds Bank Review*, No. 65, July 1962, pp. 16-28.

'The Postwar Resurgence of the French Economy', in Stanley HOFFMANN, Charles P. KINDLEBERGER, Laurence WYLIE, Jesse R. PITTS Jean-Baptiste DUROSELLE and François GOGUEL, eds., *In Search of France*, Cambridge, Mass.: Harvard University Press, 1963; published in Great Britain as *France: Change and Tradition*, London: Victor Gollanz, pp. 118-58.

'Flexible Exchange Rates', in *Monetary Management*, A Series of Research Studies prepared for the Commission on Money and Credit, Englewood Cliffs, N. J.: Prentice-Hall, 1963, pp. 403-25.

'European Economic Integration and the Development of a Single Financial Center for Long-Term Capital', *Weltwirtschaftliches Archiv*, Band 90, Heft 2, July 1963, pp. 189-208.

'The Prospects for International Liquidity and the Future Evolution of the International Payments System', in Roy HARROD and Douglas HAGUE, eds., *International Trade Theory in a Developing World*, Proceedings of a Conference held by the International Economic Association, New York: Macmillan; Trowbridge and London: 1963, pp. 372-92.

Statement on 'Short-run measures to strengthen the dollar', in *The United States Balance of Payments*, Hearings before the Joint Economic Committee, Congress of the United States, 88th Congress, First Session, (November 12, 13, 14 and 15, 1963), Part 3: *The International Monetary System: Functioning and Possible Reform*, Washington, D.C.: United States Government Printing Office, 1963, pp. 383-89.

Economic Growth in France and Britain, 1851-1950, Cambridge Mass.: Harvard University Press; London: Oxford University Press, 1964.

'Terms of Trade for Primary Products', in Marion CLAWSON, ed., *Natural Resources and International Development*, published for Resources for the Future by Johns Hopkins Press, Baltimore,1964, pp. 339-66.

'All About United States Foreign Investment' (Book review of Raymond F. MIKESELL, ed., *United States Private and Government Investment Abroad*, Eugene, Or.: University of Oregon Press, 1962), *Economic Development and Cultural Change*, vol. XII, No. 3, April 1964, pp. 325-8.

'Reflections on the Present U.S. Position on East-West Trade', in *East-West Trade*, A compilation of Views of Businessmen, Bankers, and Academic Experts, Committee on Foreign Relations, United States Senate, 88th Congress, Second session, November 1964, Washington, D.C.: United States Government Printing Office, 1964, pp. 268-72.

'Le rôle des États-Unis dans l'économie européenne', in *L'Europe du XIXe et XXe siècle*, vol. III, Milano: Marzorati, 1964, pp. 477-51.

'Trends in International Economics', *Annals of the American Academy of Political and Social Science*, vol. 358, 'New Nations: The Problem of Political Development', March 1965, pp. 170-9.

'Balance-of-Payments Deficits and the International Market for Liquidity', *Essays in International Finance*, No. 46, May 1965, International Finance Section, Department of Economics, Princeton, N. J.: Princeton University.

'Mass Migration, Then and Now', *Foreign Affairs*, vol. 43, No. 4, July 1965, pp. 647-58.

'Emigration and Economic Growth', *Banca Nazionale del Lavoro Quarterly Review*, No. 74, September 1965, pp. 235-54.

'The United States Balance of Payments in the Nineteenth Century. A Review Article', *Explorations in Entrepreneurial History*, vol. 3, No. 1, Second Series, Fall 1965, pp. 50-5.

'The Economics of 2001', *M.I.T. Alumni Association Technology Review*, vol. 68, No. 1, November 1965, pp. 25, 26, 64.

'Germany's persistent Balance-of-Payments Disequilibrium', in R. E. BALDWIN, ed., *Trade, Growth, and the Balance of Payments*. Essays in Honour of Gottfried Haberler, Chicago, Ill.: Rand McNally; Amsterdam: North-Holland, 1965, pp. 230-48.

'Integration vs. Nationalism in the European Economy', *The Reporter*, vol. 33, No. 10, December 2, 1965, pp. 38-40.

'European Integration and the International Corporation', *Columbia Journal of World Business*, vol. 1, No. 1, Winter 1965, pp. 65-73.

Europe and the Dollar, Cambridge, Mass. and London: M.I.T. Press, 1966.

'The Dollar and World Liquidity – A minority view' (with Emile DESPRES and Walter S. SALANT), *The Economist*, vol. CCXVIII, No. 6389, 5th February 1966, pp. 526-29; reprinted, in the original version, in Charles P. KINDLEBERGER, *International Money. A collection of essays*, London: George Allan & Unwin, 1987, pp. 42-52.

'Capital Movements and International Payments Adjustment', *Konjunkturpolitik*, vol. 12, No. 1, 1966, pp. 10-30.

'International Monetary Arrangements', *The English, Scottish and Australian Bank Research Lecture*, Brisbane, Australia: University of Queensland Press, August 1966, pp. 1-20.

Statement on *Contingency Planning for U.S. International Monetary Policy*, Subcommittee on International Exchange and Payments of the Joint Economic Committee, Congress of the United States, 89th Congress, Second Session, Washington, D.C.: United States Government Printing Office, 1966, pp. 49-62.

'The Contribution of International Trade Theory to Regional Economics', in *Capital, Income and Regional Development*, Report of a Conference sponsored by the Agricultural Policy Institute and the

Department of Economics, North Carolina State University (October 1964), API Series 21 (October 1966), pp. 17-27.

'Professional Education: Toward a Way of Thought', *MIT Technology Review*, November 1966, pp. 29-32, 49, 50, 53, 54.

'The International Monetary System – Strengths, Weaknesses and Possible Improvements', in *International Financing 1966*, National Industrial Conference Board. Addresses before the Third International Financing Conference, November 22, 1966.

Europe's Postwar Growth. The Role of Labor Supply, Cambridge, Mass.: Harvard University Press; London: Oxford University Press, 1967.

Statement on 'Public Policy and the International Corporation', in *International Aspects of Antitrust*, Hearings before the Subcommittee on Antitrust and Monopoly of the Committee of the Judiciary, United States Senate, Part I, Washington, D.C.: United States Government Printing Office, 1967, pp. 148-173.

'The U.S. in World Markets', in John R. COLEMAN, ed., *The Changing American Economy*, New York and London: Basic Books, 1967, pp. 210-20.

'French Planning', in Max F. MILLIKAN, ed., *National Economic Planning*, Conference of the Universities-National Bureau of Economic Research, New York and London: Columbia University Press, 1967, pp. 279-300.

'Liberal Policies vs. Controls in the Foreign Trade of Developing Countries', *A.I.D. Discussion Paper*, No. 14, Agency for International Development, Department of State, Washington, D.C.: April 1967; reprinted in James D. THEBERGE, ed., *Economics of Trade and Development*, New York and London: John Wiley and Sons, 1968, pp. 490-505.

Statement on *The 1967 Economic Report of the President*, Hearings before the Joint Economic Committee, Congress of the United States, 90th Congress, First Session, February 20, 21 and 23, 1967, Part 4, Washington, D.C.: United States Government Printing Office, 1967 pp. 833-9; reprinted in Charles P. KINDLEBERGER, *International Money. A collection of essays*, London: George Allen & Unwin, 1981, pp. 113-19.

'The State of Economic Partnership Today', *Interplay*, vol. 1, No. 1, June-July 1967, pp. 19-21.

'A Monetary Policy for an Interdependent World', *The Lamp*, (Standard Oil Company, New Jersey) vol. 49, No. 2, New York, Summer 1967, pp. 20-2.

'The Politics of International Money and World Language', *Essays in International Finance*, No. 61, August 1967, International Finance Section, Department of Economics, Princeton, N. Y.: Princeton University; reprinted in Charles P. KINDLEBERGER, *International Money. A collection of essays*, London: George Allen & Unwin, 1981, pp. 24-34.

'The Pros and Cons of an International Capital Market', *Zeitschrift für die Gesamte Staatswissenschaft*, Band 123, Heft 4, Oktober 1967, pp. 600-17; reprinted in Charles P. KINDLEBERGER, *International Money. A collection of essays*, London: George Allen & Unwin, 1981, pp. 225-42.

'The International Firm and the International Capital Market', *Southern Economic Journal*, vol. XXXIV, No. 2, October 1967, pp. 223-30.

'Study abroad and Emigration', in Walter ADAMS, ed., *The Brain Drain*, New York: Macmillan and London: Collier-Macmillan, 1968, pp. 135-55.

'Commitment to Responsibility', *World Politics*, vol. XX, No. 2, January 1968, pp. 357-67.

Testimony on *Gold Cover*, Hearings before the Committe on Banking and Currency, United States Senate, 90th Congress, Second Session, January 30, 31 and February 1, 1968, Washington, D.C.: United States Government Printing Office, pp. 166-77.

'The Marshall Plan and the Cold War', *International Journal* (Canadian Institute of International Affairs), vol. XXIII, No. 3, Summer 1968, pp. 369-82.

American Business Abroad. Six Lectures on Direct Investment, New Haven and London: Yale University Press, 1969.

'The Euro-Dollar and the Internationalization of United States Monetary Policy', *Banca Nazionale del Lavoro Quarterly Review*, No. 88, March 1969, pp. 3-15; reprinted in Charles P. KINDLEBERGER, *International Money. A collection of essays*, London: George Allen & Unwin, 1981, pp. 100-10.

'Investissements and matières premières', *Esprit*, vol. 37, No. 380, Avril 1969, pp. 630-36.

'Is Time Money?', *Interplay*, vol. 3, No. 2, August-September 1969, pp. 40-2; reprinted in Charles P. KINDLEBERGER, *International Money. A collection of essays*, London: George Allen & Unwin, 1981, pp. 35-41).

'Princeton Essays in International Finance', *Journal of Economic Literature*, vol. VII, No. 3, September 1969, pp. 807-10.

'Measuring Equilibrium in the Balance of Payments', *Journal of Political Economy*, vol. 77, No. 6, November-December 1969, pp. 873-91; reprinted in Charles P. KINDLEBERGER, *International Money. A collection of essays*, London: George Allan & Unwin, 1981, pp. 120-38

Power and Money. The Economics of International Politics and the Politics of International Economics, London: Macmillan, 1970.

The International Corporation: A Symposium (editor), Cambridge, Mass. and London: M.I.T. Press, 1970.

'Le prix de l'or et le problème du N-1', *Économie Appliquée*, tome XXXIII, No. 1, 1970, pp. 149-62; the original English text is reprinted in Charles P. KINDLEBERGER, *International Money. A collection of essays*, London: George Allen & Unwin 1981, pp. 76-86.

'The Case for Fixed Exchange Rates, 1969', in *The International Adjustment Mechanism*, Proceedings of the Monetary Conference, October 8-10, 1969, The Federal Reserve Bank of Boston, pp. 93-108; reprinted in Charles P. KINDLEBERGER, *International Money. A collection of essays.*, London: George Allen & Unwin, 1981, pp. 169-82.

'Toward a GATT for Investment: A Proposal for Supervision of the International Corporation' (with Paul M. GOLDBERG), *Law and Policy in International Business*, vol. 2, No. 2, Summer 1970, pp. 295-325.

'Less-Developed Countries and the International Capital Market', in Jesse W. MARKHAM and Gustav F. PAPANEK, ed., *Industrial Organization and Economic Development. In Honour of E. S. Mason*, Boston: Houghton Mifflin, 1970, pp. 337-49; reprinted in Charles P. KINDLEBERGER, *International Money. A collection of essays*, London: George Allen & Unwin, 1981, pp. 243-55.

'An Economist's View of the Eurodollar Market: Two Puzzles', in Herbert V. PROCHNOW, ed., *The Eurodollar*, Chicago, Ill.: Rand McNally, 1970, pp. 257-71; reprinted in Charles P. KINDLEBERGER, *International Money. A collection of essays*, London: George Allen & Unwin, 1981, pp. 53-62.

'The Dollar System', *New England Economic Review*, Federal Reserve Bank of Boston, September-October 1970, pp. 3-9.

North American and Western European Economic Policies. Proceedings of a Conference held by the International Economic Association (joint editor with Andrew SHONFIELD), London: Macmillan, 1971.

'Optimal Economic Interdependence', in Charles P. KINDLEBERGER and Andrew SHONFIELD, eds., *North American and Western European Economic Policies*, Proceedings of a Conference held by the International Economic Association, London: Macmillan, 1971, pp. 491-502; reprinted in Charles P. KINDLEBERGER, *International Money. A collection of essays*, London: George Allen & Unwin, 1981, pp. 317-28.

'Magdoff on Imperialism, Two Views, II, *Public Policy*, vol. XIX, No. 3, Summer 1971, pp. 531-4.

'The International Monetary Politics of a Near-Great Power: Two French Episodes, 1926-1936 and 1960-1970', *Economic Notes* (Monte dei Paschi di Siena), vol. I, Nos. 2-3, 1972, pp. 30-44.

'Restrictions on Direct Investment in Host Countries', in Jagdish N. BHAGWATI and Richard S. ECKAUS, eds., Development and Planning. Essays in Honour of Paul Rosenstein-Radan, London: George Allen & Unwin, 1972, pp. 201-9.

'The Benefits of International Money', *Journal of International Economics*, vol. 2, No. 4, September 1972, pp. 425-42; reprinted in Charles P. KINDLEBERGER, *International Money. A collection of essays*, London: George Allen & Unwin, 1981, pp. 9-23.

'Direct Investment in Less-Developed Countries: Historical Wrongs and Present Values', in Luis Eugenio DI MARCO, ed., *International Economics and Development*, Essays in Honour of Raúl Prebisch, New York and London: Academic Press, 1972, pp. 387-402.

'Memorandum for the Fily: Origins of the Marshall Plan' (July 22, 1948); published in Washington, D.C.: 1972o *see* in this *Bibliography*, p. 141.

The World in Depression, 1929-1939, Berkeley: University of California Press; London: Allen LANE, The Penguin Press, 1973; Revised and enlarged edition, Berkeley: University of California Press, 1986.

'Money Illusion and Foreign Exchange', in C. Fred BERGSTEN and William G. TYLER, eds., *Leading Issues in International Economic Policy*. Essays in Honour of George N. Halm, Lexington, Mass.: Lexington

Books, D.C. Heath, 1973, pp. 51-64; reprinted in Charles P. KIN-DLEBERGER, *International Money. A collection of essays*, London: George Allen & Unwin, 1981, pp. 87-99.

'Imperialism', in Robert B. CARSON, Jerry INGLES and Douglas McLAUD, eds., *Government in the American Economy. Conventional and Radical Studies on the Growth of State Economic Power*, Lexington, Mass.: D.C. Heath, 1973, pp. 474-83.

'The Formation of Financial Centers. A Study in Comparative Economic History', *Princeton Studies in International Finance*, No. 36, November 1974, International Finance Section, Department of Economics, Princeton, N. J.: Princeton University.

'The Dollar – Yesterday, Today and Tomorrow', in J. BACKMAN and E. BLOCK, eds., *Multinational Corporations, Trade and the Dollar in the Seventies*, with a Foreward by Harold S. GENEEN, New York: New York University Press, 1974, pp. 21-39.

'Origins of United States Direct Investment in France', *Business History Review*, Special Issue 'Multinational Enterprise', vol. XLVIII, No. 3, Autumn 1974, pp. 382-413.

'Economic Integration via External Markets and Factors', in Willy SELLEKAERTS, ed., *International Trade and Finance*. Essays in Honour of Jan Tinbergen, London, Macmillan, 1974, pp. 103-16.

'Size of Firm and Size of Nation', in John H. DUNNING, ed., *Economic Analysis and the International Enterprise*, London: George Allen & Unwin, 1974, pp. 342-62.

'The Multinational Corporation in a World of Militant Developing Countries', in George W. Ball, ed., *Global Companies*, Englewood Cliffs, N. Y.: Prentice-Hall (The American Assembly.), 1975, pp. 70-84.

'Economia al bivio', in *Il Caso Italiano* with Fabio Luca CAVAZZA and Stephen R. GRAUBARD, Milano: Garzanti Editore, 1975, pp. 241-70.

'The SDR as international monev', in Paul COULBOIS, ed., Essais en l'honneur de Jean Marchal, vol. 2: *La Monnaie*, Paris: Editions Cujas, 1975, pp. 303-14.

'Germany's Overtaking of England, 1806-1914', Part I: *Weltwirtschaftliches Archiv*, Band 111, Heft 2, 1975, pp. 253-81; Part II: *Weltwirtschaftliches Archiv*, Band 111, Heft 3, 1975, pp. 477-504.

'The Rise of Free Trade in Western Europe, 1820-1875', *Journal of Economic History*, vol. XXXV, No. 1, March 1975, pp. 20-55.

'Quantity and Price, Especially in Financial Markets', *Quarterly Review of Economics and Business*, vol. 15, No. 2, Summer 1975, pp. 7-19; reprinted in Charles P. KINDLEBERGER, *International Money. A collection of essays*, London: George Allen & Unwin, 1981, pp. 256-68.

'World Populism', Atlantic Economic Journal, vol. III, No. 2, November 1975, pp. 1-7.

'Commercial Expansion and the Industrial Revolution', *Journal of European Economic History*, vol. 4, No. 3, Winter 1975, pp. 613-54.

'Lessons of Floating Exchange Rates', in Karl BRUNNER and Allan H. MELTZER, eds, *Institutional Arrangements and the Inflation Problem*, Amsterdam, New York and Oxford: North-Holland, 1976, pp. 51-77; reprinted in Charles P. KINDLEBERGER, *International Money. A collection of essays*, London: George Allen & Unwin, 1981, pp. 183-206.

'Technical Education and the French Entrepreneur', in Robert FORSTER and Joseph N. MOODY, eds., *Enterprise and Entrepreneurs in Nineteenth – and Twentieth-Century France*, with an introduction by Edward C. CARTER II, Baltimore and London: Johns Hopkins University Press, 1976, pp. 3-39.

'Systems of International Economic Organization', in David P. CALLEO, ed., *Money and the Coming World Order*, New York: New York University Press, 1976, pp. 15-39.

'International Financial Intermediation for Developing Countries', in Ronald I. MCKINNON, ed., *Money and Finance in Economic Growth and Development*. Essays in Honor of Edward S. Shaw, New York and Basel: Marcel Dekker, 1976, pp. 127-37; reprinted in Charles P. KINDLEBERGER, *International Money. A Collection of essays*, London: George Allen & Unwin, 1981, pp. 269-78.

'The Exchange-Stability Issue at Rambouillet and Jamaica', in Edward M. BERNSTEIN *et al.*, *Reflections on Jamaica*, Essays in International Finance, no. 115, April 1976, International Finance Section, Department of Economics, Princeton, N. J.: Princeton University, pp. 25-9.

'The International Monetary System', the *E. S. Woodward Lectures*, given at the University of British Columbia in March 1976 and published separately by the University; reprinted in Charles P. KINDLEBERGER, *International Money. A collection of essays*, London: George Allen & Unwin, 1981, pp. 317-28.

153

'Germany's Persistent Balance-of-Payments Disequilibrium Revisited', *Banca Nazionale del Lavoro Quarterly Review*, No. 117, June 1976, pp. 118-50; reprinted in Charles P. KINDLEBERGER, *International Money. A Collection of essays*, London: George Allen & Unwin, 1981, pp. 139-68.

Multinational from Small Countries (joint editor with Tamir AGMON), Cambridge, Mass. and London: M.I.T. Press, 1977.

America in the World Economy, in Foreign Policy Association Headline Series, New York, 1977.

'The Use of Libraries by Economists: A Personal View', in Mark PERLAMN, ed., *The Organization and Retrieval of Economic Knowledge*. Proceedings of a Conference held by the International Economic Association at Kiel, West Germany, London: Macmillan, 1977, pp. 15-45.

'Les origines des investissements directs des États Unis en France', in *Association Française des Historiens Économistes. La position internationale de la France. Aspects Économiques et financiers XIXe-XXe siècles*. Textes réunis et présentés par Maurice LEVY-LEBOYER. Deuxième Congrès National. Paris et Nanterre, 5-6 Octobre 1973, Paris: Editions de l'École des Hauts Études en Sciences Sociales, 1977.

'U.S. Foreign Economic Policy, 1776-1976', *Foreign Affairs*, vol. 55, No. 2, January 1977, pp. 395-417.

'Egon Sohmen: In memoriam', *Journal of International Economics*, vol. 7, No. 3, August 1977, pp. 307-8.

Economic Response. Comparative Studies in Trade, Finance, and Growth, Cambridge, Mass. and London: Harvard University Press, 1978.

Manias, Panics, and Crashes. A History of Financial Crises, London: Macmillan; New York: Basic Books, 1978.

The Aging Economy, Bernhard-Harms-Vorlesungen, No. 8, Kiel: Institut für Weltwirtschaft an der Universität Kiel, 1978; reprinted in *Weltwirtschaftliches Archiv*, Band 114, Heft 3, 1978, pp. 407-21.

'Government and International Trade', *Princeton Essays in International Finance*, No. 129, July 1978, International Finance Section, Department of Economics, Princeton, N. J.: Princeton University.

'Machlup on Economic Integration', in Jacob S. DREYER, ed., *Breadth and Depth in Economics. Fritz Machlup – The Man and His Ideas*, Lexington, Mass.: D.C. Heath, 1978, pp. 301-12.

'The Historical Background: Adam Smith and the Industrial Revolution', in Thomas WILSON and Andrew S. SKINNER, eds., *The Market and the State*. Essays in Honour of Adam Smith, Oxford: Clarendon Press, 1978, pp. 1-24.

'The OECD and the Third World', in *From Marshall Plan to Global Interdependence: New Challenges for the Industrialized Nations*, Paris: OECD, 1978, pp. 105-21.

'Debt Situation of the Developing Countries in Historical Perspective', in Stephen H. GOODMAN, ed., *Financing and Risk in Developing Countries*, New York: Praeger, 1978, pp. 3-11; reprinted in *Aussenwirtschaft*, vol. 36, Heft 4, December 1981, pp. 372-82.

'The Twentieth Century Fontana' (Review article), *Journal of Economic History*, vol. XXXVIII, No. 3, September 1978, pp. 729-33.

Two Hundred Years of Franco-American Relations, Papers of the Bicentennial Colloquium of the Society of French Historical Studies, in Newport, Rhode Island, September 7-10, 1979 (published in 1983), pp. 121-50.

'Is Symmetry Possible in International Money?', in Harry I. GREENFIELD, Albert M. LEVENSON, William HAMOVITCH, and Eugene ROTWEIN, eds., *Theory for Economic Efficiency*: Essays in Honor of Abba P. Lerner, Cambridge, Mass. and London: M.I.T. Press, 1979, pp. 63-75.

'The International Causes and Consequences of the Great Crash', *Journal of Portfolio Management*, vol. 6, No. 1, Fall 1979, pp. 11-14.

'Government Policies and Changing Shares in World Trade', *American Economic Review*, vol. 70, No. 2, Papers and Proceedings of the Ninety-Second Annual Meeting of the American Economic Association (Atlanta, Georgia, December 28-30, 1979) edited by George H. BORTS and Daniel F. SPULBER, May 1980, pp. 293-8.

'The Life of an Economist', *Banca Nazionale del Lavoro Quarterly Review*, No. 134, September 1980, pp. 231-45.

Review of *The Collected Works of Walter Bagehot: The Economic Essays*, vols. 9, 10, and 11, edited by Norman St JOHN-STEVAS, *Journal of Economic Literature*, vol. XVIII, No. 1, March 1980, pp. 118-21.

Review of *Causality in Economics* by Sir John HICKS and of *Looking into the seeds of time: Social Mechanisms in Economic Development*, by Y. S. BRENNER, *Journal of Economic Literature*, vol. XVIII, No. 3, September 1980, p. 1086-8.

'Keynesianism vs. Monetarism in Eighteenth- and Nineteenth-Century France', *History of Political Economy*, vol. 12, No. 4, Winter 1980, pp. 499-523.

'Responsability in Economic Life', *Lloyds Bank Review*, No. 138, October 1980, pp. 1-11.

'Myths and Realities of Forward-Exchange Markets', in John S. CHIPMAN and Charles P. KINDLEBERGER, eds., *Flexible Exchange Rates and the Balance of Payments*. Essays in Memory of Egon Sohmen, Amsterdam, New York and Oxford: North-Holland, 1980, pp. 127-38.

'The Rise and Fall of the United States in the World Economy', in *The Business Cycle and Public Policy*, A Compendium of Papers, Joint Economic Committee, November 28, 1980, Washington, D.C.: United States Government Printing Office, pp. 67-79.

Flexible Exchange Rates and the Balance of Payments. Essays in Memory of Egon Sohmen (joint editor with John S. CHIPMAN), Studies in International Economics, vol. 7, Amsterdam, New York and Oxford: North-Holland, 1980.

International Money. A collection of essays, London: Allen & Unwin, 1981.

'Debt Situation of Developing Countries in Historical Perspective (1800-1945)', *Aussenwirtschaft*, vol. 36, Heft 4, Sonder nummer: 'Längerfristige Aspekte der internationalen Verschuldung von Entwicklungs ländern, Dezember 1981, pp. 372-80.

'Historical Perspective on the Decline in U.S. Productivity', in *Dimensions of Productivity Research*, Proceedings of the Conference on Productivity Research, the American Productivity Center, Houston, Texas, April 21-24, 1980, edited by John D. HOGAN and Anna M. CRAIG, vol. 1, Houston, Tx: American Productivity Center, 1981, pp. 715-24.

'Relazione di apertura', BANCO DI ROMA, *Banca e Industria fra le due guerre*, Bologna: Il Mulino, 1981, pp. 85-95.

'Interim Report on the Rail Movement of German Reserves' (June 16, 1944); published in Austin, Tx: 1981; *see* in this *Bibliography*, p. 141.

'Memorandum from E. G. Collado to Mr Clayton: "United States Foreign Policy towards Europe and its Economic Implications"' (February 25, 1946) published in Austin, Tx: 1981; *see* in this *Bibliography*, p. 141.

Financial Crises. Theory, history, and policy (joint editor with Jean-Pierre LAFFARGUE), Cambridge: Cambridge University Press; Paris: Editions de la Maison des Sciences de l'Homme, 1982.

'British Financial Reconstruction, 1815-22 and 1815-25', in Charles P. KINDLEBERGER and Guido Di TELLA, eds., *Economics in the Long View*. Essays in Honour of W. W. Rostow. vol. 3, *Applications and cases*, Part II, London: Macmillan, 1982, pp. 105-20.

Economics in the Long View. Essays in Honour of W. W. Rostow, Vol. 1: *Models and Methology*; vols. 2 and 3: *Applications and Cases*, Parts 1 and II (joint editor with Guido di TELLA), London: Macmillan, 1982.

'The Cyclical Pattern of Long-Term Lending', in Mark GERSOVITZ, Carlos F. DIAZ-ALEJANDRO, Gustav RANIS and Mark R. ROSENWEIG, eds., *The Theory and Experience of Economic Development*. Essays in Honour of Sir W. Arthur Lewis, London: George Allen & Unwin, 1982, pp. 300-12.

'Sweden in 1850 as an "Impoverished Sophisticate". Comment' (on 'Banking and Growth in Sweden before World War I'), *Journal of Economic History*, vol. XLII, No. 4, December 1982, pp. 918-20.

'International Monetary Reform in the Nineteenth Century', in *The International Monetary System under Flexible Exchange Rates*. Essays in Honour of Robert Triffin, Cambridge, Mass.: Ballinger, 1982, pp. 203-15.

'Assets and Liabilities of International Economics: The Postwar Bankruptcy of Theory and Policy', *Economic Notes*, (Monte dei Paschi di Siena), 1982, No. 2, pp. 47-66.

The Multinational Corporation in the 1980s (joint editor with David B. AUDRETCH), Cambridge, Mass. and London: M.I.T. Press, 1983.

'1929: Ten Lessons for Today', *Challenge*, March/April 1983, vol. 26, No. 1, pp. 58-61.

'Key Currencies and Financial Centers', in Fritz MACHLUP, Gerhard FELS, and Hubertus MULLER-GROELING, eds., *Reflections on a Troubled World Economy*: Essays in Honour of Herbert Giersch, London: Macmillan, 1983, pp. 75-90.

'Standards as Public, Collective and Private Goods', *Kyklos*, vol. 36, No. 3, 1983, pp. 377-96.

'The World Economic Showdown since the 1970s', in Helmut KRA-

MER and Felix Butsohek, eds., *Strukturpolitik als Dimension der Vollbe-schäftigungspolitik*, Stuttgart: Gustav Fisher Verlag, 1983, pp. 11-25

A Financial History of Western Europe, London: George Allen & Unwin, 1984.

Multinational Excursions, Cambridge, Mass. and London: M.I.T. Press, 1984.

'Was Adam Smith a Monetarist or a Keynesian?', *Business Economics*, vol. 19, No. 1, January 1984, pp. 5-12.

'Financial Institutions and Economic Development: A Comparison of Great Britain and France in the Eighteenth and Nineteenth Centuries', *Explorations in Economic History*, vol. 21, No. 2, April 1984 pp. 103-124.

'Banking and Industry between the two Wars: An International Comparison', *Journal of European Economic History*, vol. 13, No. 2, Fall 1984, pp. 7-28.

'International Trade and National Prosperity', *Cato Journal*, vol. 3, No. 3, Winter 1983/1984, pp. 623-37.

'International Banks as Leaders or Followers of International Business: An Historical Perspective', *Journal of Banking and Finance*, vol. 7, No. 4, December 1984, pp. 583-95.

Keynesianism vs. monetarism and other essays in financial history. London: George Allen & Unwin, 1985.

'The Importance of free Trade in Developing Countries', *Indian Journal of Quantitative Economics*, vol. 1, No. 1, 1985, pp. 45-60.

'Losing Information: The More We Study the Gold Standard the Less We Know about It', *Weltwirtschaftliches Archiv*, Band 121, Heft 2, 1985, pp. 382-6.

'Multinational Ownership of Shipping Activities', *World Economy*, vol. 8, No. 3, September 1985, pp. 249-65.

'The Dollar Yesterday, Today, and Tomorrow', *Banca Nazionale del Lavoro Quarterly Review*, No. 155, December 1985, pp. 295-308.

'Historical Perspective on Today's Third-World Debt Problem, *Economies et Sociétés*, vol. 19, No. 9, September 1985, pp. 109-34.

'My Working Philosophy', *American Economist*, vol. XXI, No. 1, Spring 1986, pp. 13-20.

'International Public Goods without International Government', *American Economic Review*, vol. 76, No. 1, March 1986, pp. 1-13.

'Reversible and Irreversible Processes in Economics', *Challenge*, vol. 29, No. 4, September/October 1986, pp. 4-10.

'Hierarchy versus Inertial Cooperation', *International Organization*, vol. 40, No. 4, Autumn 1986, pp. 841-7.

Marshall Plan Days, London and Boston: George Allen & Unwin, 1987.

International Capital Movements, based on the Marshall Lectures given at the University of Cambridge in 1985, Cambridge: Cambridge University Press, 1987.

The International Economic Order. Essays on Financial Crisis and International Public Goods, London: Wheat sheaf: Cambridge, Mass.: M. I.T. Press, 1988.

REFERENCES

For references to Professor Kindleberger's own works quoted in the Lectures, see his complete Bibliography, pp. 141-59.

ABRAHAMS Paul P., *The Foreign Expansion of American Finance and its Relationship to the Foreign Economic Policies of the United States, 1907-1921*, New York: Arno Press, 1974.

ARRIGHI Giovanni, 'Labor Supplies in Historical Perspective: A Study of Proletarization of the African Peasantry in Rhodesia', in Giovanni ARRIGHI and John S. SAUL, eds., *Essays on the Political Economy of Africa*, New York and London: Monthly Review Press, 1973, pp. 180-236.

ARRIGHI Giovanni and John S. SAUL (eds), *Essay on the Political Economy of Africa*, New York and London: Monthly Review Press, 1973.

BAGEHOT Walter, *Lombard Street. A description of the Money Market*, London: H. S. King, 1873; reprinted in *The Collected Works of Walter Bagehot*, edited by Norman St John-STEVAS, London: The Economist, 1978, vol. IX, pp. 45-233.

BAGEHOT Walter, 'Investments', *Inquirer*, vol. XI, No. 526, July 31 1852, p. 482; reprinted in *The Collected Works of Walter Bagehot*, *op. cit.*, vol. IX, pp. 272-5.

BAGEHOT Walter, 'The Effects of the Resumption of Specie Payments in France on the Price of Silver', in *The Silver Question*, IV, *The Economist*, vol. XXXIV, March 18 1876; reprinted in *The Collected Works of Walter Bagehot*, *op. cit.*, vol. X, pp. 150-5.

BAGEHOT Walter, 'Bimetallism', in *The Silver Question*, XVII, *The Economist*, vol. XXXIV, December 30 1876; reprinted in *The Collected Works of Walter Bagehot*, *op. cit.*, vol. X, pp. 215-17.

BAGEHOT Walter, *A Universal Money (A Practical Plan for assimilating the English and American money, as a step towards a Universal Money)*, London: Longmans, 1869; reprinted in *The Collected Works of Walter Bagehot*, *op. cit.*, vol. XI, pp. 57-104.

BAGEHOT Walter, 'The Postulates of English Political Economy. No. 1', *Fortnightly Review*, No. CX, N. S., February 1 1876, pp. 215-42; reprinted in *The Collected Works of Walter Bagehot*, *op. cit.*, vol. XI, pp. 222-54.

BAGEHOT Walter, 'Adam Smith and Our Modern Economy', in *Economic Studies*, edited by Richard Holt Hutton, London: Longmans, First edition 1880, Second edition 1888; reprinted in *The Collected Works of Walter Bagehot*, *op. cit.*, vol. XI, pp. 298-328.

BAGEHOT Walter, *The Collected Works of Walter Bagehot*, edited by Norman ST JOHN-STEVAS, vols. 9-11: *The Economic Essays* with an Introduction by R. S. Sayers, London: The Economist, 1978.

BAGWELL Philip SIDNEY, *The Transport Revolution from 1770*, New York: Barnes & Noble, 1974.

BARBOUR Violet, 'Dutch and English Merchant Shipping in the Seventeenth Century', *Economic History Review*, vol. II, No. 1, January 1930, pp. 261-90; reprinted in Warren C. SCOVILLE and J. CLAYBORN LA FORCE, eds., *The Economic Development of Western Europe*, Lexington, Mass.: D. C. Heath, 1970, vol. II.

BELL Daniel, *The Coming of Post-Industrial Society: A Venture in Social Forecasting*, New York: Basic Books, 1973; London: Heinemann, 1974.

BHAGWATI Jagdish Natwarlal (ed.), *Economics and World Order, from 1970s to the 1990s*, New York: Macmillan, 1972.

BRAUDEL Fernand, *Afterthoughts on Material Civilization and Capitalism*, Baltimore: John Hopkins University Press, 1977 (translated by Patricia M. RANUM).

BRAUN Rudolf, *Sozialer und kultureller Wandel in einem ländlichen Industriebiet*, Erlenbach-Zurich: Eugen Rentsch, 1965.

BURK Kathleen, 'J. M. Keynes and the Exchange Rate Crisis of July 1917', *Economic History Review*, vol. XXXII, No. 3, August 1979, pp. 405-16.

Business History Review, Special Issue 'Multinational Enterprise', vol. XLVIII, No. 3, Autumn 1974.

CARLSON Sune, 'Company Policies for International Expansion: The Swedish Experience', in Tamir AGMON and Charles P. KINDLEBERGER, eds., *Multinationals from Small Countries*, Cambridge, Mass.: M.I.T. Press. 1977.

CHANDLER Alfred D., *Strategy and Structure. Chapters in the History of the Industrial Enterprise*, Cambridge, Mass. and London: M.I.T. Press, 1962.

CHEVALIER Michel, *Lettres sur l'Amérique du Nord*, Third edition, Paris: Gosselin, vols. 1 and 2, 1838.

CHEVALIER Michel, *On the Probable Fall in the Value of Gold: The Commercial and Social Consequences which may Ensue, and the Measures which it Invites*, Manchester: Alexander Ireland & Co; London: W. H. Smith and Son; Edinburgh: Adam and Charles Black, Third edition, 1859 (translated from the French, with Preface, by Richard COBDEN).

CLAPHAM Sir John, *The Bank of England: A History*, two vols., Cambridge: Cambridge University Press, 1945.

CLAY Sir Henry, *Lord Norman*, London: Macmillan, 1957.

CLARK Colin, *The Conditions of Economic Progress*, New York: St Martin's Press, 1940 (3rd edition, 1957).

CLARK Colin, *The Economics of 1960*, London: Macmillan, 1942.

Collected Works of Walter Bagehot, see BAGEHOT Walter.

CORTI Count Egon Caesar, *The Rise of the House of Rothschild*, translated from the German by Brian and Beatrix LUNN, *Der Aufstieg des Hauses Rothschild, 1770-1830*, Leipzig, 1927), New York: Blue Ribbon; London: Gollanz, 1928.

CRISP Olga, 'Labour and Industrialization in Russia', in Peter MATHIAS and Moisei Mikhail POSTAN, eds., *The Cambridge Economic History of Europe*, vol. VII, *The Industrial Economies: Capital, Labour, and Enterprise*, Part 2: The United States, Japan, and Russia, Cambridge: Cambridge University Press, 1978, pp. 308-415.

DARDEL Pierre, *Commerce, industrie et navigation à Rouen et au Havre au XVIIIᵉ siècle. Rivalité croissante entre ces deux ports*, Rouen: Société Libre d'Émulation de la Seine-Maritime, 1966.

DAVIS Ralph, *The Rise of the Atlantic Economies*, Ithaca: Cornell University Press, 1973.

DENISON Edward Fulton, *Why Growth Rates Differ. Postwar Experience in Nine Western Countries*, Washington, D.C.: Brookings Institution, 1967.

DE ROOVER Raymond Adrien, *Gresham on Foreign Exchange*, Cambridge, Mass.: Harvard University Press, 1949.

DE ROSA Luigi, *Iniziativa e capitale straniero nell'industria metalmeccanica del Mezzogiorno, 1840-1904*, Napoli: Giannini Editore, 1968.

DE VRIES Jan, *Barges and Capitalism. Passenger Transportation in the Dutch Economy, 1632-1839*, Wageningen: A.A.G. Bijdragen, 1978.

DIAZ-ALEJANDRO Carlos, 'The post 1971 international financial system and the less developed Countries', in Jagdish Natwarlal Bhagwati ed., *Economics and World Order, from the 1970s to the 1990s*, New York: Macmillan, 1972; also in Gerald K. HELLEINER, *A World Divided. The Less Developed Countries in the International Economy*, Cambridge: Cambridge University Press, 1976.

DI TELLA Guido, *The Economic History of Argentina, 1914-1933*, Dissertation, Massachusetts Institute of Technology, 1960.

DOLLINGER Philippe, *The German Hansa*, translated from the German and edited by D. S. AULT and S. H. STEINBERG, Stanford: Stanford University Press; London: Macmillan (original 1964), 1970.

DOMAR Evsey D., 'The Causes of Slavery or Serfdom: A Hypothesis', *Journal of Economic History*, vol. xxx, No. 1, March 1970, pp. 18-32.

DORNIC François, *L'industrie textile dans le Maine et ses débouches internationales (1630-1815)*, Le Mans: Editions Pierre-Belon, 1955.

EINAUDI Luigi, 'Teoria della moneta immaginaria nel tempo da Carlomagno alla Rivoluzione francese', *Rivista di Storia Economica*, vol. 1, 1936, pp. 1-35; translated by Giorgio TAGLIACOZZO as 'The Theory of Imaginary Money from Charlemagne to the French Revolution', in Frederick Chapin LANE and Jelle C. RIEMERSMA, eds., *Entreprise and Secular Change. Readings in Economic History*, Homewood, Ill.: Richard D. Irwin, 1953, pp. 229-61.

EMDEN Paul H., *Money Powers of Europe in the Nineteenth and Twentieth Centuries*, New York: D. Appleton-Century, 1938.

ENGELS Friedrich, *The Condition of the English Working Classes in 1848*, London: Allen & Unwin, 1892.

EVANS David Morier, *The History of the Commercial Crisis, 1857-1858, and the Stock Exchange Panic of 1859*, London: Groombridge & Sons, 1859; reprinted New York: Augustus M. Kelley, 1969.

FEI John C. H., and Gustav RANIS, *Development of the Labor Surplus Economy. Theory and Policy*, Homewood, Ill.: Richard D. Irwin, 1964.

FETTER Frank Whitson, *Development of British Monetary Orthodoxy, 1797-1875*, Cambridge, Mass.: Harvard University Press, 1965.

FETTER Frank Whitson, *The Economist in Parliament, 1780-1868*, Durham, N.C.: Duke University Press, 1980.

FISHER Allan George Barnard, 'Economic Implications of Material Progress', *International Labour Review*, July 1935, pp. 5-18.

FISHER Allan George Barnard, 'Production, Primary, Secondary and Tertiary', *Economic Record*, vol. xv, No. 28, June 1939, pp. 24-38.

FOGEL Robert William and Stanley L. ENGERMAN, *Time on the Cross*, vols. 1 and 11, Boston: Little, Brown, 1974.

FOGEL Robert William and Stanley L. ENGERMAN, 'Explaining the Relative Efficiency of Slave Agriculture in the Antebellum South, Reply', *American Economic Review*, vol. 70, No. 4, September 1980, pp. 672-90.

Fox Edward Whiting, *History in Geographic Perspective. The other France*, New York: W. W. Norton & Co., 1971.

GALBRAITH John Kenneth, *The New Industrial State*, Boston: Houghton Mifflin; London: Hamish Hamilton, 1967.

GERSCHENKRON Alexander, 'Economic Backwardness in Historical Perspective', in Berthold Frank HOSELITZ, ed., *The Progress of Underdeveloped Areas*, Chicago: University of Chicago Press, 1952; reprinted in Alexander GERSCHENKRON, *Economic Backwardness in Historical Perspective*, Cambridge, Mass.: Harvard University Press, 1962, pp. 5-30.

GERSCHENKRON Alexander, *Economic Backwardness in Historical Perspective. A Book of Essays*, Cambridge, Mass.: Harvard University Press, 1962.

GERSCHENKRON Alexander, *An Economic Spurt That Failed. Four Lectures in Austrian History*, Princeton: Princeton University Press, 1977.

GIRARD Louis, 'Transport', in John Hrothgar HABAKKUK and Moisei Mikhail POSTAN, *The Cambridge Economic History of Europe*, vol. VI, *The Industrial Revolution and After: Incomes, Population and Technological Change*, Cambridge: Cambridge University Press, 1965, pp. 212-73.

GORDON Robert Aaron, 'Rigor and Relevance in a Changing Institutional Setting', *American Economic Review*, vol. 66, No. 1, March 1976, pp. 1-14.

GOUBERT Pierre, *Familles marchands sous l'Ancien Régime: Danse et les Motte, de Beauvais*, Paris: S.E.V.P.E.N., 1959.

GRAHAM Frank Dunstone and Charles Raymond WHITTLESEY, *Golden Avalanche*, Princeton N. J.: Princeton University Press, 1939; reprinted New York: Arno Press, 1979.

HABAKKUK Hrothgar John, *American and British Technology in the Nineteenth Century. The Search for Labour-Saving Inventions*, Cambridge: Cambridge University Press, 1962.

HABAKKUK Hrothgar John, 'Family Structure and Economic Change in Nineteenth-Century Europe', *Journal of Economic History*, vol. XV, No. 1, March 1955, pp. 1-12.

HABAKKUK John H. and Moisei Mikhail POSTAN, *The Cambridge Economic History of Europe*, vol. VI, *The Industrial Revolution and After: Incomes, Population and Technological Change*, Cambridge: Cambridge University Press, 1968.

HARDACH Gerd, *The First World War, 1914-1918*, Berkeley: University of California Press, 1977.

HECKSCHER Eli Filip, 'The Bank of Sweden in its Connection with the Bank of Amsterdam', in J. G. VAN DILLEN, ed., *History of the Principal Public Banks*, The Hague: Martinus Nijhoff, 1934, pp. 161-89.

HELLEINER K. Gerald, 'Introduction', in *A World Divided. The Less Developed Countries in the International Economy*, edited by Gerald K. HELLEINER, Cambridge: Cambridge University Press, 1976, pp. 1-28.

HICKS John R., 'Monetary Theory and History: An Attempt at Perspective', in Hicks John R., *Critical Essays in Monetary Theory*, Oxford: Clarendon Press, 1967.

HICKS John R., *Critical Essays in Monetary Theory*, Oxford: Clarendon Press, 1967.

HIRSCHMAN Albert O., *The Strategy of Economic Development*, New Haven: Yale University Press, 1958.

HOSELITZ Berthold Frank (ed.), *The Progress of Underdeveloped Areas*, Chicago: University of Chicago Press, 1952.

HOUTHAKKER Hendrik S., 'An International Comparison of Household Expenditure Patterns. Commemorating the Centenary of Engel's Law', *Econometrica*, vol. 25, October 1957, pp. 532-51.

HOUTHAKKER Hendrik S., 'New Evidence on Demand Elasticities', *Econometrica*, vol. 31, April 1965, pp. 277-88.

HUFBAUER Gary C. and F. Michael ADLER, *Overseas Manufacturing Investment and the Balance of Payments*, Tax Policy Research Study, No. 1, Washington, D.C.: United States Treasury Department, 1968.

HYMER Stephen H., *The International Operations of National Firms: A Study of Direct Foreign Investment*, Ph. D. thesis, Massachusetts Institute of Technology, 1960; published Cambridge, Mass.: M.I.T. Press, 1976.

IMLAH Albert H., *Economic Elements in the Pax Britannica*, Cambridge, Mass.: Harvard University Press, 1958.

INSTITUT FÜR WELTWIRTSCHAFT UND SEEVERKEHR AN DER UNIVERSITÄT KIEL, *Der deutsche Aussenhandel unter der Einwirkung weltwirtschaftlicher Strukturwandlungen*, (vol. 20 of the *Ausschuss zur Untersuchung der Er-*

zeugungs-und Abstazbedingungen der deutschen Wirtschaft), Berlin: E. S. Mittler & Sohn, 1932.

ISARD Walter, 'The General Theory of Location and Space Economy', *Quarterly Journal of Economics*, vol. LXIII, No. 4, November 1949, pp. 476-506.

KEYNES John Maynard, 'National Self-Sufficiency', *Yale Review*, vol. XXII, No. 4, June 1933, pp. 755-69; and also in *The New Statesman and Nation*, 8th and 15th July 1933; reprinted in *The Collected Writings of John Maynard Keynes*, vol. XXI, *Activities 1931-1939: World Crisis and Policies in Britain and America*, London: Macmillan, 1982, pp. 233-46.

KEYNES John Maynard, *A Treatise on Money*: vol. I, *The Pure Theory*: vol. II, *The Applied Theory*, London: Macmillan, 1930; reprinted in *The Collected Writings of John Maynard Keynes*, respectively, vols. V and VI, London: Macmillan, 1971.

KEYNES John Maynard, *Essays in Persuasion*, London: Macmillan, 1931; reissued London: Rupert Hart-Davis, 1951; reprinted with additions in *The Collected Writings of John Maynard Keynes*, vol. IX, London: Macmillan, 1972.

KEYNES John Maynard, 'Economic Possibilities for Our Grandchildren', *Nation and Athenaeum*, 11th and 18th October 1930; reprinted in *Essays in Persuasion*, London: Macmillan, 1931; New York: Harcourt Brace and Co., 1932; also reprinted in *The Collected Writings of John Maynard Keynes*, vol. IX, London: Macmillan, 1972, pp. 321-32.

KOCKA Jürgen, *Unternehmungsverwaltung und Angestelltenschaft am Beispiel SIEMENS*, Stuttgart: Ernst Klett Verlag, 1969.

KRANTZ Frederick and Paul M. HOHENBERG, *Failed Transitions to Modern Industrial Society. Renaissance Italy and Seventeenth Century Holland*, Montreal: Interuniversity Center for European Studies, 1975.

KRAUSE Lawrence B. and Hugh T. PATRICK (eds). *Mineral Resources in the Pacific Area*. San Francisco: Federal Reserve Bank of San Francisco, 1978.

League of Nations, Economic, Financial and Transit Department, *The Course and Control of Inflation. A Review of Monetary Experience in Europe after World War I*. A Report written by Ragnar Nurkse. League of Nations, 1946.

LESER Conrad Emmanuel Victor, 'Forms of Engel Functions', *Econometrica*, vol. 31, October 1963, pp. 693-703.

LEWIS William Arthur, 'Economic Development with Unlimited Supplies of Labour', *Manchester School of Economic and Social Studies*, vol. XXII, No. 2, May 1954, pp. 139-91.

LINDERT Staffan Burenstam, *The Harried Leisure Class*, New York: Columbia University Press, 1970.

LINDERT Peter H., 'Key Currencies and Gold, 1900-1913', *Princeton Studies in International Finance*, Department of Economics, Princeton University, Princeton, N. J., No. 24, August 1969.

LOYD Samuel Jones (Lord OVERSTONE), *Reflections Suggested by a Perusal of Mr. J. Horsley Palmer's pamphlet on the Causes and Consequences of the Pressure on the Money Market*, London: Pelham Richardson, 1837.

McCLOSKEY Donald N., 'Does the Past Have Useful Economics?', *Journal of Economic Literature*, vol. XIV, No. 2, June 1976, pp. 434-61.

McKINNON Ronald I., *Money and Capital in Economic Development*, Washington, D. C.: Brookings Institution, 1973.

McNEILL William Hardy, *Greece: American Aid in Action, 1947-1956*, New York: Twentieth Century Fund, 1957.

MAGEE Stephen P., 'Three Simple Tests of the Stolper-Samuelson Theorem', in *Issues in International Economics*, edited by Peter Morris OPPENHEIMER, Stocksfields: Oriel Press, 1978, pp. 138-53.

MAGEE Stephen and Norman I. ROBINS, 'The Raw Materias Product Cycle', in Lawrence B. KRAUSE and Hugh T. Patrick, eds., *Mineral Resources in the Pacific Area*, San Francisco: Federal Reserve Bank of San Francisco, 1978, pp. 30-55; "Comments", pp. 57-68.

MARSHALL Alfred, *Money, Credit and Commerce*, London: Macmillan, 1923.

MARX KARL, *Capital: A Critique of Political Economy* (translated by Ben FOWKES, with an introduction by Ernest MANDEL), vol. I, Harmondsworth: Penguin, 1976.

MATHIAS Peter and Moisei Mikhail POSTAN (eds), *The Cambridge Economic History of Europe*, vol. VII, *The Industrial Economies: Capital, Labour, and Enterprise*, Part 1: *Britain, France, Germany, and Scandinavia;* Part 2: *The United States, Japan, and Russia*, Cambridge: Cambridge University Press, 1978.

MENDELS Franklin F., 'Proto-Industrialization: The First Phase of the Process of Industrialization', *Journal of Economic History*, vol. XXX, No. 1, March 1972, pp. 241-61.

MEYER John R., 'An Input-Output Approach to Evaluating the Influence of Exports on British Industrial Production in the late 19th Century', *Explorations in Entrepreneurial History*, vol. VIII, October 1955, pp. 12-34.

MILL John Stuart, *Principles of Political Economy, with Some of Their Applications to Social Philosophy*, First edition in two volumes, London: John W. Parker, 1848; The edition quoted in the lectures is the text edited by W. J. Ashley, London: Longman Green & Co., 1909.

MINISTÈRE DES FINANCES ET MINISTÈRE DE L'AGRICULTURE, DU COMMERCE ET DES TRAVAUX PUBLICS, *Enquête sur les principes et les faits généraux qui régissent la circulation monétaire et fiduciaire*, Paris: Imprimerie Impériale, 1867, tome II, Testimony of Garnier-Pages.

MINSKY Hyman, *John Maynard Keynes*, New York: Cambridge University Press, 1975.

MOKYR Joel, *Industrialization in the Low Countries, 1795-1850*, New Haven and London: Yale University Press, 1976.

MOLLIEN François Nicolas, *Mémories d'un Ministre du Trésor Public, 1780-1815*, Paris: Fournier, 1845, tome III.

MUNDELL ROBERT A., 'A Theory of Optimum Currency Areas', *American Economic Review*, vol. LI, No. 4, September 1961, pp. 657-64.

MYRDAL Gunnar, *An International Economy. Problems and Prospects*, London: Macmillan; New York: Harper and Brothers 1956.

New York Herald, 'The Revolution of 1857 – Its Causes and Results', in *The History of the Commercial Crisis, 1857-1858*, edited by D. MORIER EVANS, London: Groombridge & Sons, 1859.

NIEHANS Jürg, 'Benefits of Multinational Firms for a Small Parent Economy: The Case of Switzerland', in Agmon TAMIR and Charles P. KINDLEBERGER, eds., *Multinationals from Small Countries*, Cambridge, Mass.: MIT Press, 1977, pp. 1-39.

NURKSE Ragnar. *The Course and Control of Inflation. A Review of Monetary Experience in Europe after World War I.* A Report, League of Nations, 1946.

O'BRIEN Denis Patrick, 'Introduction', in *The Correspondence of Lord Overstone*, Cambridge: Cambridge University Press, 1971.

O'BRIEN Patrick and Caglar KEYDER, *Economic Growth in Britain and France, 1780-1914. Two Paths to the Twentieth Century*, London: George Allen & Unwin, 1978.

OFFICER Lawrence H., 'The Purchasing-Power-Parity Theory of Exchange Rates: A Review Article', *International Monetary Fund Staff Papers*, vol. XXIII, No. 1, March 1976, pp. 1-60.

OPPENHEIMER Peter Morris (ed.), *Issues in International Economics*, Stocksfields: Oriel Press, 1978.

PASINETTI Luigi, 'A New Theoretical Approach to the Problem of Economic Growth', *Ponteficiæ Academiæ Scientiarum Scripta Varia*, No. 28, 1965, pp. 571-696; reprinted in PASINETTI Luigi, *The Econometric Approach to Development Planning*, Amsterdam: North-Holland, 1965.

PASINETTI Luigi, *Structural Change and Economic Growth*, Cambridge: Cambridge University Press, 1981.

POLANYI Karl, *The Great Transformation*, New York: Farrar and Rinchart, 1944.

POLLARD Sidney, 'Labour in Great Britain', in Peter MATHIAS and Moisei Mikhail POSTAN, eds., *The Cambridge Economic History of Europe*, vol. VII, *The Industrial Economies: Capital, Labour, and Enterprise*, part 1, *Britain, France, Germany, and Scandinavia*, Cambridge: Cambridge University Press, 1978, pp. 97-179.

POSTHUMA Suardus, 'The International Monetary System, *Banca Nazionale del Lavoro Quarterly Review*, no. 66, Sept. 1963, pp. 239-61.

POTTER David M., *People of Plenty. Economic Abundance and the American Character*, Charles R. Walgreen Foundation Lectures, Chicago: University of Chicago Press, 1954.

RIESMAN David, *The Lonely Crowd. A Study of the Changing American Character*, New Haven: Yale University Press, 1950.

ROEHL Richard, 'French Industrialization: A Reconsideration', *Explorations in Economic History*, vol. XIII, No. 3, July, 1976, pp. 233-81.

ROSTOW Walt Whitman, *The Stage of Growth*, Cambridge: Cambridge University Press, 1960.

RUEFF Jacques and Fred HIRSCH, 'The Role and Rule of Gold: An Argument', *Princeton Essays in International Finance*, No. 47, June 1965, Department of Economics, Princeton University.

SALANT Walter S. *et al.*, *The Balance of Payments of the United States in 1968*, Washington, D. C.: Brookings Institution, 1963.

SANDBERG Lars G., 'Banking and Economic Growth in Sweden before World War I', *Journal of Economic History*, vol. XXXVIII, No. 3, September 1978, pp. 650-80.

SCHUMACHER, E. F., *Small is Beautiful. A Study of Economics as if People Mattered*, New York: Harper & Row; London: Blond Briggs, 1973.

SCOVILLE Warren C. and J. Clayborn LA FORCE (eds), *The Economic Development of Western Europe*, Lexington, Mass.: D. C. Heath, 1970.

SERVAN-SCHREIBER Jean-Jacques, *The American Challenge*, New York: Atheneum, 1968.

SHAW EDWARD STONE, *Financial Deepening in Economic Development*, New York: Oxford University Press, 1973.

SHERWIG John M., *Guineas and Gunpowder. British Foreign Aid in the Wars with France, 1793-1814*, Cambridge, Mass.: Harvard University Press, 1969.

SMART William, *Economic Annals of the Nineteenth Century*, vol. 1, *1801-1820*, vol. 2, *1821-1830*, London: Macmillan, 1910-1917; reprinted New York: Augustus M. Kelley, 1964.

SMITH Adam, *An Inquiry into the Nature and Causes of the Wealth of Nations*, two volumes, London: Printed for W. Strahan and T. Cadell, 1766. The edition quoted in the lectures is the text edited by Edwin CANNAN and published by Methuen and Co., London: Fourth edition, 1935.

SMITH Stanley Cyril, 'Metallurgy as Human Experience'. The 1974 Distinguished Lectureship in Materials and Society', *Metallurgical Transactions*, vol. LXXII, No. 4, April 1975, pp. 606-14.

SPOONER Frank C., *The International Economy and Monetary Movements in France, 1493-1725*, Cambridge, Mass.: Harvard University Press, 1972.

STEVAS ST JOHN Norman, ed., *The Collected Works of Walter Bagehot*, London: The Economist, 1978, vols. 9-11: *The Economic Essays*, with an introduction by R. S. Sayers.

STIGLER George, 'The Early History of Empirical Studies of Consumer Behavior', *Journal of Political Economy*, vol. 62, No. 2, 1954, pp. 95-113.

SUNKEL Osvaldo, 'Latin American Under development in the Year 2000', in Jagdish Natwarlal Bhagwati, ed., *Economics and World Order, from the 1970s to the 1990s*, New York: Macmillan, 1972, pp. 199-231.

SUPPLE Barry E., *Commercial Crisis and Change in England, 1600-1642. A Study in the Instability of a Mercantile Economy*, Cambridge: Cambridge University Press, 1959.

TAIRA Koji, 'Factory Labour and the Industrial Revolution in Japan', in Peter MATHIAS and Moisei Mikhail POSTAN, eds., *The Cambridge Economic History of Europe*, vol. VII, *The Industrial Economies: Capital, Labour, and Enterprise*. Part 2, *The United States, Japan, and Russia*, Cambridge: Cambridge University Press, 1978, pp. 166-214.

THOMPSON Edward Palmer, 'Time, Work-Discipline and Industrial Capitalism', *Past and Present, a journal of historical studies*, No. 38, December 1967, pp. 56-97.

TINBERGEN Jan, *International Economic Integration*, Second revised edition, Amsterdam: Elsevier Publishing Company, 1965.

TRIFFIN Robert, *Gold and the Dollar Crisis. The Future of Convertibility*, New Haven: Yale University Press, 1960.

TYSZYNSKI, H., "World Trade in Manufactured Commodities, 1899-1950", *Manchester School of Economic and Social Studies*, vol. XIX, No. 3, September 1951, pp. 272-304.

UNITED STATES SENATE, *International Monetary Conference*, held in Paris, in August, 1878, under the auspices of the Ministry of Foreign Affairs of the Republic of France, Senate Executive Document No. 58, 45th Congress, 3rd Session, Washington, D. C.: Government Printing Office, 1879.

VACIAGO Giacomo, 'Alternative Theories of Growth and the Italian Case', *Banca Nazionale del Lavoro Quarterly Review*, vol. XXIII, No. 93, June 1970, pp. 180-211.

VAN DILLEN J. G., 'The Bank of Amsterdam', in J. G. VAN DILLEN, ed., *History of the Principal Public Banks*, The Hague: Martinus Nijhoff, 1934, pp. 79-123.

VILAR Pierre, *A History of Gold and Money, 1450-1920* (translated from the 1969 French edition by Judith White), London: NLB, 1976 (first published as *Oro y Moneda en la Historia (1450-1920)*, Barcelona: Ediciones Ariel, 1969).

WALRAS Leon, *Etudes d'économie politique appliquée*, Paris: Pichon, 1898.

WAN Henry Y., "Manpower, Industrialization and Export-led Growth – The Taiwan Experience", in YUAN-LI and KUNG-CHIA YEH, eds., 'Growth, Distribution and Social Change. Essays on the Economy of the Republic of China', *Occasional Papers | Reprints*

Series in Contemporary Asian Studies, vol. xv, No. 3, 1978, published by the School of Law, University of Maryland, pp. 161-91.

WEBER Eugen, *Peasants into Frenchmen. The Modernization of Rural France, 1870-1914*, Stanford, Cal.: Stanford University Press, 1976.

WICKSELL Knut, *Lectures on Political Economy*, vol. II, *Money*, with an Introduction by Lionel Robbins, London: Macmillan, 1900.

WILKINS MIRA, *The Emergence of Multinational Enterprise: American Business Abroad from the Colonial Era to 1914*, Cambridge, Mass.: Harvard University Press, 1970.

WILLIAMSON John G., *Karl Helfferich, 1872-1924. Economist, Financier, Politician*, Princeton, N. J.: Princeton University Press, 1971.

WOLOWSKI Ludwig (Louis) FRANCISZEK Michal Rajmund, *La Question Monétaire*, Second edition, Paris: Guillaumin, 1869.

ZYMELMAN Manuel, *The Economic History of Argentina, 1933-1952*, Dissertation, Massachusetts Institute of Technology, 1958.

INDEX

INDEX

179

RAFFAELE MATTIOLI LECTURES

RAFFAELE MATTIOLI FOUNDATION
Fondazione Raffaele Mattioli
per la Storia del Pensiero Economico

Published

RICHARD F. KAHN, *The Making of Keynes' General Theory* (First edition, May 1984; Japanese edition, Tokyo: Iwanami Shoten Publishers, 1987)

FRANCO MODIGLIANI, *The Debate over Stabilization Policy* (First edition, July 1986).

CHARLES P. KINDLEBERGER, *Economic Laws and Economic History* (First edition: December 1989).

To be published

PETER MATHIAS, *The Industrial Revolution in England.*

ERIK F. LUNDBERG, *The Development of Swedish and Keynesian Macroeconomic Theory and its Impact on Economic Policy.*

NICHOLAS KALDOR, *Causes of Growth and Stagnation in the World Economy.*

SHIGETO TSURU, *Institutional Economics Revisited.*

RICHARD STONE, *Some British Empiricists in the Social Sciences.*

KARL BRUNNER - ALLAN H. MELTZER, *Money and the Economy. Issues in Monetary Analysis.*

ALAN PEACOCK, *Public Choice Analysis in Historical Perspective.*